one-dish meals

microwave cooking library®

by barbara methven

microwave cooking library®

"What's a one-dish meal?" We think it's any complete, nutritious and satisfying meal served in a single container. When you think about it, that covers a variety of popular dishes.

There's the casserole, of course. For this book, we've reinvented some old favorites, created some speedy ones and simplified make-aheads.

How about a full-meal salad? With some of these recipes, you can eat the bowl as well as the salad. Don't forget soups and stews. Here you'll find soups that microwave in a flash and others that simmer slowly on the back burner. The all-American stir-fry is faster, easier and totally new in taste.

The biggest surprise in this surprising book is the one-plate microwave meal. It doesn't look like a one-dish meal. The protein, vegetable and starch aren't mixed together, but you assemble, cook and serve them on a single plate.

Barbara Methven

CREDITS:
Design & Production: Cy DeCosse Incorporated
Art Director: Yelena Konrardy
Project Director: Peggy Ramette
Project Manager: Deborah Bialik
Home Economists: Peggy Ramette, Ann Stuart, Grace Wells
Dietitian: Patricia D. Godfrey, R.D.
Consultants: Susanne C. Mattison, Beatrice A. Ojakangas
Editors: Janice Cauley, Bernice Maehren
Director of Development Planning & Production: Jim Bindas
Production Manager: Amelia Merz
Electronic Publishing Analyst: Kevin D. Frakes
Production Staff: Joe Fahey, Peter Gloege, Melissa Grabanski, Jim Huntley, Mark Jacobson, Duane John, Daniel Meyers, Linda Schloegel, Greg Wallace, Nik Wogstad
Studio Manager: Rebecca Boyle
Photographers: Rex Irmen, John Lauenstein, Mark Macemon, Charles Nields, Mette Nielsen, Mike Parker, Cathleen Shannon
Food Stylists: Sue Brue, Bobbette Destiche, Melinda Hutchison, Amy Peterson
Color Separations: Scantrans
Printing: R. R. Donnelley & Sons (1191)

CY DE COSSE INCORPORATED
Chairman: Cy DeCosse
President: James B. Maus
Executive Vice President: William B. Jones

Library of Congress Cataloging-in-Publication Data

Methven, Barbara
  One-dish meals / Barbara Methven.

  p.   cm. — (Microwave cooking library)
Includes index.
ISBN 0-86573-572-7

  1. Microwave cookery 2. Casserole cookery I. Title. II. Series.
TX832.M41575   1991   91-24312
641.5'882 — dc20

Additional volumes in the Microwave Cooking Library series are available from the publisher:

- Basic Microwaving
- Recipe Conversion for Microwave
- Microwaving Meats
- Microwave Baking & Desserts
- Microwaving Meals in 30 Minutes
- Microwaving on a Diet
- Microwaving Fruits & Vegetables
- Microwaving Convenience Foods
- Microwaving for Holidays & Parties
- Microwaving for One & Two
- The Microwave & Freezer
- 101 Microwaving Secrets
- Microwaving Light & Healthy
- Microwaving Poultry & Seafood
- Microwaving America's Favorites
- Microwaving Fast & Easy Main Dishes
- More Microwaving Secrets
- Microwaving Light Meals & Snacks
- Holiday Microwave Ideas
- Easy Microwave Menus
- Low-fat Microwave Meals
- Cool Quick Summer Microwaving
- Ground Beef Microwave Meals
- Microwave Speed Meals
- One Pound of Imagination: Main Dishes

Contents

What You Need to Know Before You Start

All around the world, home-style family cooking relies on one-dish meals. In America, one-dish meals are enjoying renewed popularity because they fit a dining style that favors reduced portions of meat and greater emphasis on other protein sources, such as vegetables and grains.

One-dish meals make menu planning easy. The protein, vegetable and starch components complement one another. A balanced one-dish meal also simplifies nutrition planning.

If your only idea of a one-dish meal is a casserole, or "hot dish," this book has some surprises for you. In our book, a one-dish meal is any complete, nutritious and satisfying meal served in one dish. They don't all have to look and taste like casseroles.

How to Use This Book

The recipes in this book offer satisfying meals served in single containers, and are prepared using one of four different approaches, each with very different results.

One-plate Meals. This may be the ultimate one-dish meal... the protein, vegetable and starch components are assembled, cooked and served on the same plate. To achieve this meal conventionally, you'd have to cook all the components separately and arrange them on the plate just before serving. With a microwave oven, you place the foods on a plate, cover with plastic wrap and microwave without stirring, rearranging or turning over.

American Stir-fry. The fast and easy stir-fry just got faster and easier, with a distinctly American accent. Microwaving eliminates most of the stirring as well as the fat of frying. This versatile cooking method adapts to a variety of popular tastes, including Southern, Tex-Mex and Italian, as well as Oriental.

Casseroles. We haven't neglected the casserole, one of the easiest and best-loved one-dish meals. In fact, casseroles offer so many possibilities that this chapter is divided into three sections.

Healthy Classics updates old favorites like Mac and Cheese by reducing fat, sodium and calories while retaining the taste you remember. For those who want to modernize these casseroles further, there are variations that include vegetables.

Speedy Casseroles cut down the time you spend in the kitchen by using the microwave oven and some canned and convenience foods for shortcut preparation. Final heating may be done by either microwave or conventional methods.

Make-ahead Casseroles are designed to mellow in the refrigerator for at least half a day. Making them ahead is not only convenient, it's an essential part of preparation. Don't bother to cook the pasta; mix it into the casserole dry and let time do the work.

Soups & Stews. Few dishes satisfy such diverse tastes as soups and stews. They can be light and refreshing or hearty and comforting. Some of these recipes microwave quickly and serve as an easy, nourishing meal for up to four people. For larger quantities, simmer the soup conventionally using one of our homemade bean or pasta soup and seasoning mixes. Two distinctive soup recipes accompany the directions for each mix.

Salad Bowl Meals. Add refreshing variety to your one-dish repertoire with full-meal salads. For a flourish of flavor, style and just plain fun, serve the salad in one of the edible bowls featured in this section.

Nutritional Information

All these one-dish meals have been formulated to be nutritionally balanced and complete. Following each recipe you'll find a per-serving analysis of the calorie, protein, carbohydrate, fat, cholesterol and sodium content, as well as exchanges. Where serving quantity varies, the analysis is for the greater number of servings. For example, if the dish serves four to six people, the nutritional analysis is based on six servings. Where a recipe suggests alternate ingredients, such as margarine or butter, the analysis applies to the first ingredient listed. Substituting the alternative ingredient may alter the nutritional analysis. Where variations accompany the recipe, the analysis covers the original recipe only. Optional ingredients are not included in the analysis.

Freezing & Defrosting One-dish Meals

Casseroles and soups make great freezer foods. Freeze them in family-size batches or single servings. Avoid freezing soups and casseroles made with eggs, cheese, seafood, uncooked rice and vegetables, mayonnaise and sour cream. Some ingredients, such as beans, rice, pasta and potatoes, soften when frozen, so they should be cooked only until slightly underdone. Freeze casserole toppings separately and add just before heating.

Layered foods and other dishes that cannot be stirred during reheating should be frozen in a lined casserole, as directed below. This frees the dish for other uses and saves freezer space. Also, the food will heat more quickly if placed in a dish that is at room temperature.

Soups and stirrable casseroles should be packaged in plastic freezer bags and boxes, or margarine, ice cream or deli containers with tight lids. Leave 1/4-inch head space for food expansion. Seal, label and freeze.

How to Freeze Nonstirrable Casseroles

Line baking dish with generous piece of plastic wrap. Transfer desired amount of prepared casserole to dish; freeze until firm.

Remove food from baking dish. Wrap airtight with plastic wrap, then overwrap with freezer paper or foil. Label, date and return to freezer.

Freezer-to-Table Heating Chart

Item	Servings	Power	Microwave Time
Soups and Stews	1 serving 2 servings 4 servings	High High High	6-8 minutes 11-15 minutes 23-36 minutes
Stirrable Casseroles	1 serving 2 servings 4 servings	High High High	5-7 minutes 10-13 minutes 13-25 minutes
Nonstirrable Casseroles	1 serving 2 servings 4 servings	50% (Medium) 50% (Medium) 50% (Medium)	11-22 minutes 21-25 minutes 32-45 minutes

How to Heat Frozen Soups & Stirrable Casseroles

Microwave in package at High just until food can be removed. Place food in casserole. Cover.

Microwave at High for half the time, as directed in chart. Break apart with fork.

Microwave for remaining time, or until hot, stirring once or twice.

How to Heat Frozen Nonstirrable Casseroles

Unwrap food. If plastic sticks, microwave at High just until it can be removed.

Place food in baking dish. Cover. Microwave at 50% (Medium), as directed in chart.

Rotate dish twice during heating.

One-plate Meals

Fennel Pork & Vegetables

Marinara Ravioli with Vegetables

Dilled Salmon, New Potatoes & Broccoli

One-plate Meals: Techniques

Assemble, cook and serve a complete, nutritious meal right on the dinner plate. Most of the single-serving recipes include either a piece of poultry, fish or meat, rice or pasta and vegetables. Assemble one dinner or multiply the recipe to make several. One-plate meals are an ideal solution for singles, couples and families whose members eat at different times.

You can prepare plates in advance, then cover and refrigerate them until they're needed. Add an extra minute of microwaving time for a plate that has been chilled. If you want to add more color to meats, brush them lightly with bouquet, soy, teriyaki or barbecue sauce, or sprinkle with paprika or chili powder before cooking. Since these will add their flavor to the food, choose one that is appropriate for the style of the dish.

Choose a deep, round microwave-safe dinner plate with a narrow rim. The recessed center collects juices and helps rehydrate rice or pasta. Do not use plates with metallic trim or any you are not certain are suitable for microwaving. Many manufacturers now label plates "microwave-safe."

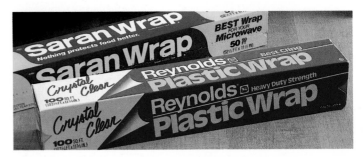

Select a premium-quality plastic wrap made specifically for use in the microwave oven.

Create your own one-plate meals using chicken, pork or fish and fresh or frozen vegetables. Include a dry carbohydrate, such as uncooked instant rice, couscous, fine egg noodles, fresh pasta or stuffing mix. Add 1 to 2 tablespoons water, sauce or gravy. Microwave about 5 minutes at High for each pound of food.

Compare a plate containing rice, which absorbs juices and excess moisture, with one that omits the dry carbohydrate. Notice the pool of juices surrounding meat and vegetables.

How to Microwave One-plate Meals

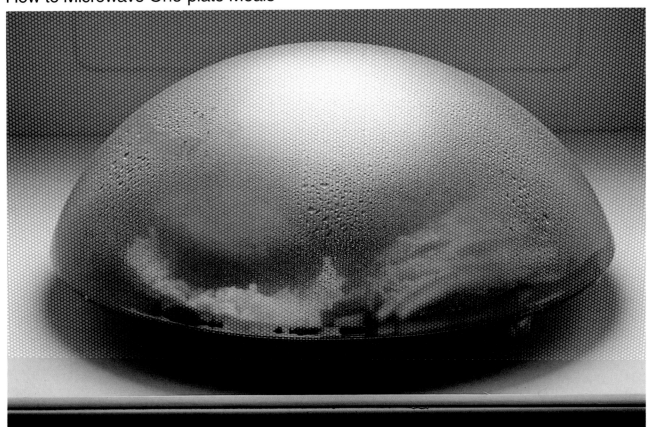

Cover the plate with a sheet of microwave plastic wrap about 1 inch larger than the diameter of the plate. Seal edges of wrap to lower side of plate rim. During microwaving, wrap domes up with steam, which cooks food evenly and holds plastic away from food. Microwave as directed in recipe, rotating dish once during cooking if your oven does not have a turntable.

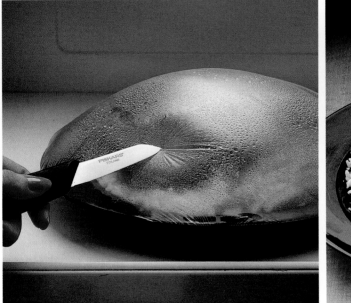

Pierce plastic wrap with tip of knife to release steam. Remove film immediately, lifting it from the edge farthest from you to avoid steam burns. If food must stand, re-cover loosely with wax paper or microwave cooking paper.

Cheese & Onion Beef Rolls ▼

- 2 tablespoons shredded Cheddar cheese
- 2 tablespoons sliced green onion
- 2 slices fully cooked roast beef
  (2 to 3 oz. each)
- 1 medium tomato, cut into 6 slices
- 1/4 teaspoon dried basil leaves
- 1/8 teaspoon garlic powder

1 serving

Sprinkle 1 tablespoon cheese and 1 tablespoon onion down center of each beef slice. Roll up tightly. Arrange tomato slices, slightly overlapping, on dinner plate. Top with beef rolls, seam-sides-down. Sprinkle with basil and garlic powder. Cover plate with plastic wrap. Microwave at High for 2 to 3 minutes, or until cheese is melted, rotating plate once. Pierce plastic wrap with tip of knife to release steam. Remove wrap.

Per Serving: Calories: 330 • Protein: 41 g. • Carbohydrate: 7 g.
• Fat: 14 g. • Cholesterol: 124 mg. • Sodium: 160 mg.
Exchanges: 5 lean meat, 1½ vegetable

Barbecue Cube Steak & Squash ▼

- 1/3 cup uncooked instant rice
- 1 beef cube steak (about 4 oz.)
- 1 tablespoon barbecue sauce
- 1/2 cup chopped green or red pepper
- 5 slices seeded acorn squash (1/2-inch slices)
- 1 tablespoon margarine or butter

1 serving

Place rice to one side on dinner plate. Top with cube steak. Spread barbecue sauce over cube steak and sprinkle with green pepper. Arrange squash slices, slightly overlapping, next to rice and meat. In small bowl, microwave margarine at High for 45 seconds to 1 minute, or until melted. Drizzle over squash. Cover plate with plastic wrap. Microwave at High for 5 to 7 minutes, or until squash is tender, rotating plate once. Pierce plastic wrap with tip of knife to release steam. Remove wrap. Before serving, fluff rice with fork.

Per Serving: Calories: 470 • Protein: 29 g. • Carbohydrate: 54 g.
• Fat: 16 g. • Cholesterol: 64 mg. • Sodium: 320 mg.
Exchanges: 3 starch, 3 lean meat, ½ vegetable, ½ fruit, ½ fat

Mini Meatloaf with Dilled Potatoes & Carrots ▼

¼ lb. extra-lean ground
  beef, crumbled
2 tablespoons milk
2 tablespoons sliced green
  onion
1 tablespoon unseasoned
  dry bread crumbs
2 teaspoons catsup
3 small new potatoes (about
  8 oz.)
½ cup frozen crinkle-cut
  carrots
1 tablespoon margarine or
  butter
½ teaspoon dried dill weed

1 serving

In small mixing bowl, combine ground beef, milk, onion, bread crumbs and catsup. Shape meat mixture into 4 x 2½-inch loaf. Place on dinner plate. Arrange potatoes and carrots on plate. In small bowl, microwave margarine and dill weed at High for 45 seconds to 1 minute, or until margarine is melted. Mix well. Spoon over potatoes and carrots. Cover plate with plastic wrap. Microwave at High for 6 to 7½ minutes, or until meat is firm and no longer pink, rotating plate once. Pierce plastic wrap with tip of knife to release steam. Remove wrap.

Per Serving: Calories: 580 • Protein: 29 g. • Carbohydrate: 57 g. • Fat: 26 g.
• Cholesterol: 73 mg. • Sodium: 440 mg.
Exchanges: 3 starch, 2 medium-fat meat, 2½ vegetable, 3 fat

Sunday Salisbury Steak Dinner

¼ lb. extra-lean ground beef, crumbled
1 tablespoon unseasoned dry bread crumbs
¼ teaspoon seasoned salt
  Dash pepper
¼ cup canned sliced mushrooms, rinsed and drained
¼ cup prepared beef gravy
½ cup frozen peas
⅓ cup water
2 tablespoons milk
2 teaspoons margarine or butter
⅛ teaspoon salt
⅓ cup instant mashed potato flakes

1 serving

In small mixing bowl, combine ground beef, bread crumbs, seasoned salt and pepper. Shape meat mixture into 4-inch patty. Place on dinner plate. Top patty with mushrooms and gravy. Arrange peas next to patty. In 6-oz. custard cup, combine remaining ingredients. Place custard cup on plate. Cover plate with plastic wrap. Microwave at High for 7 to 8 minutes, or until meat is firm and no longer pink, rotating plate once. Pierce plastic wrap with tip of knife to release steam. Remove wrap.

Per Serving: Calories: 630 • Protein: 34 g. • Carbohydrate: 70 g. • Fat: 24 g. • Cholesterol: 75 mg. • Sodium: 1450 mg. Exchanges: 4 starch, 3 lean meat, 2 vegetable, 3 fat

Porcupine Beef Patty ▲

1 pkg. (6 oz.) uncooked seasoned long-grain white and wild rice mix
¼ lb. extra-lean ground beef, crumbled
1 baking potato (about 5 oz.), cut into 8 wedges
½ cup frozen mixed vegetables
1 tablespoon margarine or butter
½ teaspoon seasoned salt

1 serving

Prepare rice as directed on package. In small mixing bowl, combine ground beef and ⅓ cup rice. Reserve remaining rice for future use. Shape meat mixture into 4-inch patty. Place in center of dinner plate. Arrange potato wedges and vegetables on plate next to patty. In small bowl, microwave margarine and seasoned salt at High for 45 seconds to 1 minute, or until margarine is melted. Spoon over potato wedges and vegetables. Cover plate with plastic wrap. Microwave at High for 5 to 7 minutes, or until meat is firm and no longer pink, rotating plate once. Pierce plastic wrap with tip of knife to release steam. Remove wrap.

Per Serving: Calories: 510 • Protein: 28 g. • Carbohydrate: 43 g. • Fat: 26 g. • Cholesterol: 71 mg. • Sodium: 1210 mg. Exchanges: 2½ starch, 3 medium-fat meat, 1 vegetable, 2 fat

14

Nacho Chips & Chili Dip ▼

⅓ to ½ cup prepared chili
½ medium green pepper, seeded
25 tortilla chips
1 cup shredded Cheddar cheese
2 tablespoons canned or fresh chopped green chilies, drained

1 serving

Spoon chili into green pepper half to within ¼ inch of top. Cover pepper with plastic wrap. Place on dinner plate. Arrange chips on plate around pepper. Sprinkle chips with cheese and green chilies. Microwave at High for 2 to 3½ minutes, or until cheese is melted and chili is warm, rotating plate once. Pierce plastic wrap with tip of knife to release steam. Remove wrap.

Per Serving: Calories: 910 • Protein: 39 g. • Carbohydrate: 60 g. • Fat: 62 g. • Cholesterol: 133 mg. • Sodium: 1590 mg.
Exchanges: 3½ starch, 3½ high-fat meat, 1½ vegetable, 6 fat

Fennel Pork & Vegetables ▼

- 2 tablespoons apple juice
- 1 tablespoon vegetable oil
- 1 teaspoon soy sauce
- ¼ teaspoon fennel seed, crushed
- ¼ teaspoon paprika
- 1 boneless pork chop (about 4 oz.)
- ½ cup shredded green cabbage
- ½ cup shredded red cabbage
- 2 tablespoons sliced green onion
- ¼ cup julienne carrot (2 × ¼-inch strips)

1 serving

In medium mixing bowl, combine juice, oil, soy sauce, fennel seed and paprika. Add pork chop, turning to coat. Set aside. On dinner plate, combine cabbage and onions. Arrange carrot around edge of cabbage mixture. Place pork chop in center. Pour marinade evenly over all ingredients. Cover plate with plastic wrap. Microwave at High for 6 to 7 minutes, or until meat is firm and no longer pink, rotating plate once. Pierce plastic wrap with tip of knife to release steam. Remove wrap.

Per Serving: Calories: 390 • Protein: 26 g. • Carbohydrate: 13 g. • Fat: 26 g.
• Cholesterol: 81 mg. • Sodium: 430 mg.
Exchanges: 3 lean meat, 1 vegetable, ½ fruit, 3½ fat

Ham & Broccoli Divan

1 slice toast, cut in half
    diagonally
2 slices fully cooked ham
    (about 1 oz. each)
2 frozen broccoli spears
2 tablespoons pasteurized
    process cheese spread

1 serving

Place toast on dinner plate. Wrap 1 slice ham around each broccoli spear. Place on toast. Cover plate with plastic wrap. Microwave at High for 2 to 3 minutes, or until broccoli is tender, rotating plate once. Pierce plastic wrap with tip of knife to release steam. Remove wrap. In small bowl, microwave cheese spread at High for 30 to 45 seconds, or until melted. Spoon over ham, broccoli and toast.

Per Serving: Calories: 280 • Protein: 22 g.
• Carbohydrate: 24 g. • Fat: 10 g.
• Cholesterol: 47 mg. • Sodium: 1250 mg.
Exchanges: 1 starch, 2 medium-fat meat, 2 vegetable

Zesty Pork & Couscous ▲

¼ cup uncooked couscous
1 tablespoon margarine or
    butter
2 tablespoons orange juice
¼ teaspoon chili powder
¼ teaspoon sugar
⅛ teaspoon salt
    Dash ground cumin
    Dash cayenne

1 boneless pork chop (about
    4 oz.), cut into 1½-inch
    strips
1 small yellow summer squash
    or zucchini, sliced (1 cup)
¼ cup chopped red onion
    Seeded chopped tomato
    (optional)

1 serving

Place couscous on dinner plate. Set aside. In medium mixing bowl, microwave margarine at High for 45 seconds to 1 minute, or until melted. Stir in juice, chili powder, sugar, salt, cumin and cayenne. Mix well. Add pork, squash and onion. Toss to coat. Spoon pork mixture over couscous. Cover plate with plastic wrap. Microwave at High for 5 to 6 minutes, or until meat is no longer pink, rotating plate once. Pierce plastic wrap with tip of knife to release steam. Remove wrap. Before serving, fluff couscous with fork. Sprinkle with tomato.

Per Serving: Calories: 550 • Protein: 32 g. • Carbohydrate: 49 g. • Fat: 25 g.
• Cholesterol: 81 mg. • Sodium: 480 mg.
Exchanges: 2 starch, 3 lean meat, 2½ vegetable, ½ fruit, 3 fat

Polish Sausages
& Caraway Sauerkraut ▲

½ cup sauerkraut, rinsed and drained,
   pressing to remove excess moisture
¼ teaspoon caraway seed
2 fully cooked Polish sausages (about 3 oz.
   each), scored at ¾-inch intervals
½ medium Rome apple, cored
   and cut into ¼-inch wedges
10 to 12 baby carrots, cut in half lengthwise
1 tablespoon packed brown sugar

1 serving

Arrange sauerkraut in center of dinner plate.
Sprinkle with caraway seed. Place sausages on
top of sauerkraut. Arrange apple wedges and
carrots next to sausages. Sprinkle evenly with
sugar. Cover plate with plastic wrap. Microwave
at High for 4 to 6 minutes, or until carrots are tender,
rotating plate once. Pierce plastic wrap with tip
of knife to release steam. Remove wrap.

Per Serving: Calories: 700 • Protein: 26 g. • Carbohydrate: 38 g.
• Fat: 49 g. • Cholesterol: 119 mg. • Sodium: 2290 mg.
Exchanges: 3 high-fat meat, 3 vegetable, 1½ fruit, 5 fat

Italian Sausages, Peppers & Potatoes

1 medium red potato, sliced (about 8 oz.)
1 cup green, red and yellow pepper strips
   (1½ × ¼-inch strips)
1 tablespoon olive oil
¼ teaspoon Italian seasoning
¼ teaspoon garlic salt
⅛ teaspoon crushed red pepper flakes
2 fully cooked Polish sausages (about 3 oz. each)

1 serving

In small mixing bowl, combine all ingredients,
except sausages. Arrange potato mixture on
plate. Place sausages on top of mixture. Cover
plate with plastic wrap. Microwave at High for 5
to 6 minutes, or until potatoes are tender, rotating
plate once. Pierce plastic wrap with tip of knife to
release steam. Remove wrap.

Per Serving: Calories: 790 • Protein: 27 g. • Carbohydrate: 30 g.
• Fat: 63 g. • Cholesterol: 119 mg. • Sodium: 1960 mg.
Exchanges: 1½ starch, 3 high-fat meat, 1½ vegetable, 7½ fat

Sunny Citrus Pancake Breakfast

½ medium pink grapefruit
3 tablespoons orange marmalade or raspberry preserves, divided
3 frozen microwave pancakes (4-inch)
2 frozen fully cooked sausage links

1 serving

Cut around edges and sections of grapefruit to loosen. Place on dinner plate. Spread top of grapefruit with 1 tablespoon marmalade. Arrange pancakes next to grapefruit. Place sausages next to pancakes. Cover plate with plastic wrap. Microwave at High for 4 to 5 minutes, or until hot, rotating plate once. Pierce plastic wrap with tip of knife to release steam. Remove wrap. Spread remaining marmalade over pancakes. Serve immediately.

Per Serving: Calories: 570
• Protein: 13 g.
• Carbohydrate: 104 g.
• Fat: 14 g.
• Cholesterol: 33 mg.
• Sodium: 1080 mg.
Exchanges: 3 starch, ½ medium-fat meat, 3½ fruit, 2 fat

Parmesan Pork with Herb-seasoned Rice & Vegetables ▼

⅓ cup uncooked instant rice
1 tablespoon water
1 boneless pork chop (about 4 oz.)
½ medium red pepper, seeded
⅓ cup frozen corn
1 small zucchini, cut into strips (3 × ¼-inch strips)
2 tablespoons shredded fresh Parmesan cheese
½ teaspoon Italian seasoning

1 serving

Place rice on dinner plate. Sprinkle with water. Place pork chop over rice. Place pepper half next to pork chop. Fill with corn. Arrange zucchini on other side of plate. Sprinkle vegetables with Parmesan cheese. Sprinkle vegetables and meat with Italian seasoning. Cover plate with plastic wrap. Microwave at High for 6 to 7 minutes, or until meat is firm and no longer pink, rotating plate once. Pierce plastic wrap with tip of knife to release steam. Remove wrap. Before serving, fluff rice with fork.

Per Serving: Calories: 530 • Protein: 42 g. • Carbohydrate: 47 g. • Fat: 20 g.
• Cholesterol: 110 mg. • Sodium: 310 mg.
Exchanges: 2 starch, 4 lean meat, 3½ vegetable, 1½ fat

Chicken & Vegetable Lo Mein

2 tablespoons teriyaki sauce
1 tablespoon peanut butter
3 tablespoons water
1 tablespoon vegetable oil
   Dash cayenne
½ boneless whole chicken breast, skin removed (about 4 oz.)
½ cup uncooked fine egg noodles (about 1½ oz.)
½ cup fresh snow pea pods, trimmed (about 2 oz.)
½ cup coarsely chopped red pepper
2 tablespoons chopped dry-roasted peanuts

1 serving

In medium mixing bowl, combine teriyaki sauce and peanut butter. Microwave at High for 30 seconds. Stir until smooth. Stir in water, oil and cayenne. Add chicken breast, turning to coat. Marinate at room temperature for 10 minutes. Place noodles on dinner plate. Spoon ¼ cup marinade over noodles. Top with pea pods and chicken. Place red pepper around edge of noodles. Pour remaining marinade over all. Cover plate with plastic wrap. Microwave at High for 5 to 6 minutes, or until meat is firm and no longer pink, rotating plate once. Pierce plastic wrap with tip of knife to release steam. Remove wrap. Cover with wax paper or microwave cooking paper. Let stand for 5 minutes. Before serving, fluff noodles with fork. Sprinkle with peanuts.

Per Serving: Calories: 680 • Protein: 43 g. • Carbohydrate: 51 g. • Fat: 35 g.
• Cholesterol: 107 mg. • Sodium: 1680 mg.
Exchanges: 2½ starch, 4½ lean meat, 1 vegetable, ½ fruit, 4 fat

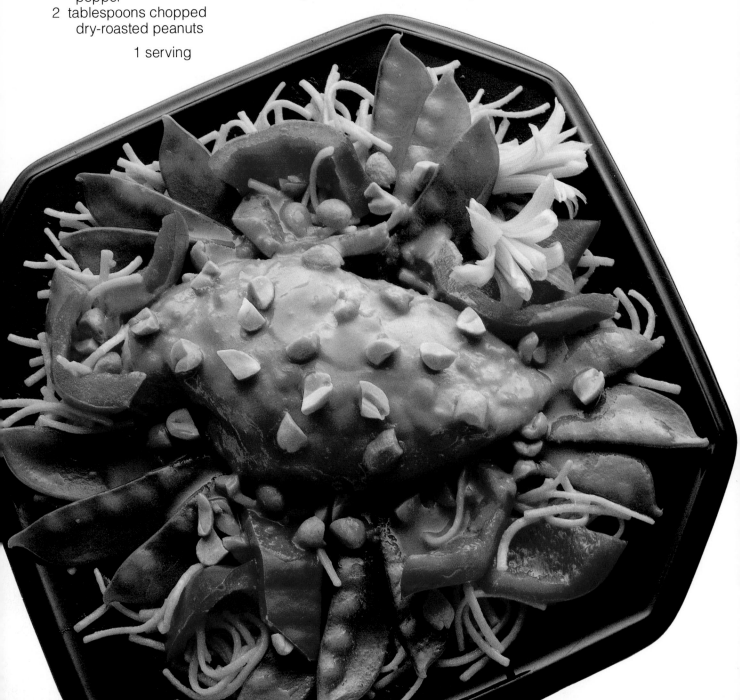

Citrus Herbed Chicken & Rice with Vegetables

1/3 cup uncooked instant rice
2 tablespoons water
1 teaspoon grated lemon or orange peel
1/8 teaspoon dried thyme leaves
1/8 teaspoon dried rosemary leaves
   Dash garlic powder, salt and pepper
1/2 boneless whole chicken breast, skin removed (about 4 oz.)
1 cup frozen cauliflower, zucchini, carrots and red pepper

1 serving

Place rice to one side on dinner plate. Sprinkle with water. In small bowl, combine peel and seasonings. Sprinkle half of seasoning mixture over rice. Place chicken breast on top of rice. Sprinkle with remaining seasoning mixture. Arrange vegetables next to chicken breast and rice. Cover plate with plastic wrap. Microwave at High for 5 to 6 minutes, or until meat is firm and no longer pink, rotating plate once. Pierce plastic wrap with tip of knife to release steam. Remove wrap. Before serving, fluff rice with fork.

Per Serving:
Calories: 280
• Protein: 28 g.
• Carbohydrate: 34 g.
• Fat: 3 g.
• Cholesterol: 67 mg.
• Sodium: 220 mg.
Exchanges:
1½ starch,
2½ lean meat,
2 vegetable

Lemon Basil Chicken & Vegetables ▼

1/3 cup uncooked instant rice
2 tablespoons water
1 small carrot
1 small zucchini
1 tablespoon margarine or butter
1 teaspoon grated lemon peel
1/4 teaspoon dried basil leaves
1/2 boneless whole chicken breast, skin removed (about 4 oz.)

1 serving

Place rice on dinner plate. Sprinkle with water. Using vegetable peeler, cut lengthwise ribbons from carrot and zucchini, discarding center portions of vegetables. Arrange vegetables over rice. Set aside. In small bowl, microwave margarine at High for 45 seconds to 1 minute, or until melted. Add peel and basil. Mix well. Place chicken breast over vegetables. Drizzle margarine mixture over chicken breast. Cover plate with plastic wrap. Microwave at High for 4 to 5 minutes, or until meat is firm and no longer pink, rotating plate once. Pierce plastic wrap with tip of knife to release steam. Remove wrap. Before serving, fluff rice with fork.

Per Serving: Calories: 410 • Protein: 30 g. • Carbohydrate: 40 g. • Fat: 15 g.
• Cholesterol: 67 mg. • Sodium: 230 mg.
Exchanges: 1½ starch, 2½ lean meat, 3½ vegetable, 1½ fat

Southern Chicken Dinner

1 tablespoon margarine or
   butter
3 tablespoons water
½ cup corn bread stuffing mix
1 cup frozen broccoli cuts
½ cup canned black-eyed
   peas, rinsed and drained
¼ cup frozen corn
2 tablespoons canned
   chopped green chilies
2 chicken pieces (2 to 3 oz.
   each), skin removed
¼ teaspoon dried thyme
   leaves
¼ teaspoon paprika

1 serving

In small mixing bowl, microwave margarine at High for 45 seconds to 1 minute, or until melted. Stir in water and stuffing mix. On dinner plate, combine stuffing mixture, broccoli, peas, corn and chilies. Place chicken pieces over vegetables and stuffing. Sprinkle with thyme and paprika. Cover plate with plastic wrap. Microwave at High for 6 to 7 minutes, or until meat is firm and no longer pink, rotating plate once. Pierce plastic wrap with tip of knife to release steam. Remove wrap. Before serving, fluff stuffing mixture with fork.

Per Serving: Calories: 700 • Protein: 45 g. • Carbohydrate: 84 g. • Fat: 22 g.
• Cholesterol: 78 mg. • Sodium: 1420 mg.
Exchanges: 4½ starch, 3½ lean meat, 3 vegetable, 2 fat

Chicken Fajita

½ boneless whole chicken breast (about 4 oz.), skin removed, cut into 1½-inch pieces
1 small onion, sliced and separated into rings (½ cup)
½ cup green pepper strips (1½ × ¼-inch strips)
½ cup red pepper strips (1½ × ¼-inch strips)
¼ cup prepared fajita sauce
2 flour tortillas (8-inch)

1 serving

In medium mixing bowl, combine all ingredients, except tortillas. Spoon mixture onto dinner plate. Cover plate with plastic wrap. Microwave at High for 4 to 5 minutes, or until meat is firm and no longer pink, rotating plate once. Pierce plastic wrap with tip of knife to release steam. Remove wrap.

Place flour tortillas between damp paper towels. Microwave at High for 20 to 30 seconds, or until tortillas are warm to the touch. Place half of chicken mixture in each warm tortilla. Roll up tortilla. Serve with salsa, sour cream and guacamole, if desired.

Per Serving: Calories: 490 • Protein: 32 g. • Carbohydrate: 67 g.
• Fat: 10 g. • Cholesterol: 67 mg. • Sodium: 920 mg.
Exchanges: 3 starch, 2½ lean meat, 4 vegetable, ½ fat

Variation:
Beef Fajita:
Follow recipe above, except substitute 4-oz. boneless beef sirloin, cut into 1½-inch pieces, for chicken. Cover with plastic wrap. Marinate at room temperature for 15 minutes. Continue with recipe as directed.

Southwestern Chicken & Rice ▼

⅓ cup uncooked instant rice
½ boneless whole chicken breast (about 4 oz.),
   skin removed, cut into 1½-inch pieces
1 small onion, sliced and separated into rings
   (½ cup)
½ cup green pepper strips (1½ × ¼-inch strips)
½ cup red pepper strips (1½ × ¼-inch strips)
¼ cup prepared fajita sauce

1 serving

Place rice on dinner plate. In medium mixing
bowl, combine remaining ingredients. Spoon
chicken mixture over rice. Cover plate with plastic wrap. Microwave at High for 5 to 6 minutes,
or until meat is firm and no longer pink, rotating
plate once. Pierce plastic wrap with tip of knife
to release steam. Remove wrap. Before serving,
fluff with fork.

Per Serving: Calories: 320 • Protein: 28 g. • Carbohydrate: 43 g.
• Fat: 3 g. • Cholesterol: 67 mg. • Sodium: 520 mg.
Exchanges: 1½ starch, 2½ lean meat, 4 vegetable

Sicilian Chicken

1 frozen fully cooked breaded chicken patty
   (about 3 oz.)
2 tablespoons spaghetti sauce
1 slice mozzarella cheese (1 oz.)
2 frozen broccoli spears
⅛ teaspoon Italian seasoning

1 serving

Place chicken patty to one side on dinner plate.
Top with spaghetti sauce and cheese. Place
broccoli next to chicken. Sprinkle chicken and
broccoli with Italian seasoning. Cover plate with
plastic wrap. Microwave at High for 3 to 4 minutes,
or until cheese is melted and broccoli is tender-
crisp, rotating plate once. Pierce plastic wrap
with tip of knife to release steam. Remove wrap.

Per Serving: Calories: 410 • Protein: 29 g. • Carbohydrate: 24 g.
• Fat: 23 g. • Cholesterol: 49 mg. • Sodium: 1170 mg.
Exchanges: 3 lean meat, 4½ vegetable, 3 fat

Turkey & Vegetable Stuffing Dinner

2 slices fully cooked turkey breast (2 to 3 oz. each)
¼ cup prepared turkey gravy
1 tablespoon margarine or butter
3 tablespoons water
½ cup frozen mixed vegetables
½ cup herb-seasoned stuffing mix

1 serving

Place turkey slices to one side on dinner plate. Pour gravy over turkey. Set aside. In medium mixing bowl, microwave margarine at High for 45 seconds to 1 minute, or until melted. Add water, vegetables and stuffing mix. Mix well. Spoon stuffing mixture next to turkey. Cover plate with plastic wrap. Microwave at High for 5 to 6 minutes, or until hot, rotating plate once. Pierce plastic wrap with tip of knife to release steam. Remove wrap.

Per Serving: Calories: 630 • Protein: 46 g. • Carbohydrate: 63 g. • Fat: 21 g.
• Cholesterol: 90 mg. • Sodium: 1520 mg.
Exchanges: 3½ starch, 4 lean meat, 2 vegetable, 2 fat

Layered Turkey Dinner

1 tablespoon margarine or
   butter
½ cup herb-seasoned stuffing
   mix
2 tablespoons hot water
1 tablespoon canned sliced
   mushrooms
2 slices fully cooked turkey
   breast (2 to 3 oz. each)
5 fresh Brussels sprouts, cut
   into quarters
1 tablespoon cranberry sauce

1 serving

In small mixing bowl, microwave margarine at High for 45 seconds
to 1 minute, or until melted. Add stuffing mix, water and mushrooms.
Mix well. Place 1 slice turkey on dinner plate. Spoon stuffing mixture
over turkey slice. Top with remaining turkey slice. Arrange Brussels
sprouts on plate. Cover plate with plastic wrap. Microwave at High
for 4 to 6 minutes, or until Brussels sprouts are tender and meat is
hot, rotating plate once. Pierce plastic wrap with tip of knife to release
steam. Remove wrap. Top with cranberry sauce.

Per Serving: Calories: 580 • Protein: 47 g. • Carbohydrate: 66 g. • Fat: 15 g.
• Cholesterol: 97 mg. • Sodium: 1200 mg.
Exchanges: 3 starch, 4½ lean meat, 2½ vegetable, ½ fruit

Dijon Turkey & Rice Dinner

- ⅓ cup uncooked instant brown rice
- ¼ cup chopped red or green pepper
- ¼ cup frozen corn
- 1 tablespoon margarine or butter
- 2 teaspoons Dijon mustard
- 1 teaspoon lemon juice
- 1 teaspoon honey
- ⅛ teaspoon dried thyme leaves
  Dash salt
- ¼ cup water
- 4 - oz. fresh turkey tenderloin, cut into ¼-inch slices
- 4 oz. fresh asparagus spears

1 serving

On dinner plate, combine rice, red pepper and corn. Spoon evenly over surface of plate. In 1-cup measure, microwave margarine at High for 45 seconds to 1 minute, or until melted. Stir in mustard until smooth. Stir in juice, honey, thyme, salt and water. Mix well. Pour ¼ cup mustard mixture evenly over rice mixture on plate. Toss to coat. Arrange turkey and asparagus over rice. Drizzle remaining mustard mixture over turkey. Cover plate with plastic wrap. Microwave at High for 6 to 7 minutes, or until meat is firm and no longer pink, rotating plate once. Pierce plastic wrap with tip of knife to release steam. Remove wrap. Before serving, fluff with fork.

Per Serving: Calories: 440 • Protein: 34 g.• Carbohydrate: 48 g. • Fat: 13 g.
• Cholesterol: 71 mg. • Sodium: 440 mg.
Exchanges: 2 starch, 3 lean meat, 3½ vegetable, ½ fat

Lemony Salmon Steak

- 1 salmon steak (about 6 oz.)
- 1 cup shredded iceberg lettuce
- ½ cup frozen peas
- 1 small yellow summer squash, sliced (1 cup)
- ½ fresh lemon
- 1 tablespoon margarine or butter
- 2 teaspoons lemon juice
- ¼ teaspoon sugar
- ¼ teaspoon dried tarragon leaves
- ⅛ teaspoon salt
  Dash pepper

  1 serving

Place salmon steak in center of dinner plate. On one side of salmon, combine lettuce and peas. Arrange squash slices on other side. Set aside. Carefully remove lemon pulp from lemon half, leaving shell intact. Place remaining ingredients in hollowed-out lemon half. Place on plate next to fish. Cover plate with plastic wrap. Microwave at High for 7 to 8 minutes, or until fish flakes easily with fork, rotating plate once. Pierce plastic wrap with tip of knife to release steam. Remove wrap. To serve, spoon margarine mixture over fish.

Per Serving: Calories: 400 • Protein: 34 g. • Carbohydrate: 19 g. • Fat: 21 g.
• Cholesterol: 79 mg. • Sodium: 550 mg.
Exchanges: 1 starch, 4 lean meat, 1 vegetable, 1½ fat

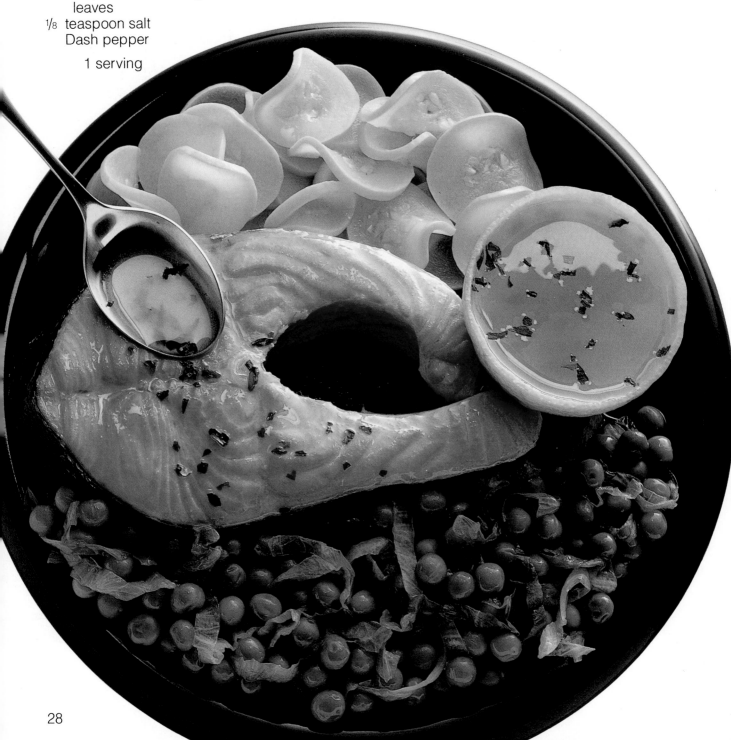

Sole with Herbed Vegetables & Rice

⅓ cup uncooked instant
    brown rice
2 tablespoons water
⅓ cup julienne carrot
    (2 × ¼-inch strips)
⅓ cup julienne zucchini
    (2 × ¼-inch strips)
⅓ cup julienne yellow summer
    squash (2 × ¼-inch strips)
1 sole fillet (about 4 oz.)
1 tablespoon margarine or
    butter
1 teaspoon grated lemon peel
¼ teaspoon Italian seasoning

1 serving

Place rice on dinner plate. Sprinkle with water. Arrange vegetables over rice. Place sole fillet over vegetables. Set aside. In small bowl, microwave margarine at High for 45 seconds to 1 minute, or until melted. Add peel and Italian seasoning. Mix well. Drizzle margarine mixture over fish. Cover plate with plastic wrap. Microwave at High for 4 to 6 minutes, or until fish flakes easily with fork, rotating plate once. Pierce plastic wrap with tip of knife to release steam. Remove wrap. Before serving, fluff with fork.

Per Serving: Calories: 360 • Protein: 25 g. • Carbohydrate: 34 g. • Fat: 13 g.
• Cholesterol: 54 mg. • Sodium: 240 mg.
Exchanges: 1½ starch, 2½ lean meat, 2 vegetable, 1 fat

Orange Scallops & Rice

  4 oz. bay scallops
 ½ cup chopped red pepper
 ⅓ cup uncooked instant rice
  1 tablespoon margarine or
     butter
  2 tablespoons water
  1 tablespoon orange juice
 ⅛ teaspoon salt
 ⅛ teaspoon ground turmeric
  1 cup packed fresh spinach
     leaves
  1 orange slice, cut in half

                    1 serving

On dinner plate, combine scallops, red pepper and rice. Set aside. In small bowl, microwave margarine at High for 45 seconds to 1 minute, or until melted. Stir in water, juice, salt and turmeric. Pour over scallop mixture. Stir to coat. Arrange spinach leaves around scallop mixture. Cover plate with plastic wrap. Microwave at High for 5 to 6 minutes, or until scallops are firm and opaque, rotating plate once. Pierce plastic wrap with tip of knife to release steam. Remove wrap. Before serving, fluff with fork. Garnish with orange slice.

Per Serving: Calories: 360 • Protein: 24 g. • Carbohydrate: 38 g. • Fat: 13 g.
• Cholesterol: 37 mg. • Sodium: 630 mg.
Exchanges: 2 starch, 2 lean meat, 1½ vegetable, 1½ fat

Dilled Salmon, New Potatoes & Broccoli

1 salmon steak (about 4 oz.)
3 small new potatoes, cut
   into quarters
3 fresh broccoli spears
1 tablespoon margarine or
   butter
1 teaspoon grated orange
   peel
½ teaspoon dried dill weed

1 serving

Place salmon steak in center of dinner plate. Arrange potatoes and broccoli on either side of salmon. In small bowl, microwave margarine at High for 45 seconds to 1 minute, or until melted. Add peel and dill weed. Mix well. Drizzle margarine mixture over fish and potatoes. Cover plate with plastic wrap. Microwave at High for 4 to 5 minutes, or until fish flakes easily with fork, rotating plate once. Pierce plastic wrap with tip of knife to release steam. Remove wrap.

Per Serving: Calories: 420 • Protein: 28 g. • Carbohydrate: 37 g. • Fat: 19 g. • Cholesterol: 59 mg. • Sodium: 220 mg.
Exchanges: 2 starch, 3 lean meat, 1½ vegetable, 2 fat

Marinara Ravioli with Vegetables

4 oz. uncooked fresh cheese
   ravioli (1 cup)
½ cup spaghetti sauce
½ cup sliced fresh mushrooms
½ cup green pepper strips
   (2 × ¼-inch strips)
1 to 3 teaspoons grated
   Parmesan cheese

1 serving

Place ravioli to one side on dinner plate. Top with spaghetti sauce. Stir gently to coat. Place mushrooms and pepper strips next to ravioli. Cover plate with plastic wrap. Microwave at High for 5 to 6 minutes, or until vegetables and ravioli are tender, rotating plate once. Pierce plastic wrap with tip of knife to release steam. Remove wrap. Cover with wax paper or microwave cooking paper. Let stand for 5 minutes. Before serving, toss vegetables gently with ravioli, if desired. Sprinkle with Parmesan cheese.

Per Serving: Calories: 490 • Protein: 17 g. • Carbohydrate: 87 g.
• Fat: 9 g. • Cholesterol: 84 mg. • Sodium: 690 mg.
Exchanges: 3½ starch, 7 vegetable, 1½ fat

Ratatouille Pasta ▼

2 oz. uncooked fresh capellini (angel hair spaghetti)
1 cup chopped eggplant
½ cup chopped green pepper
1 can (8 oz.) whole tomatoes, undrained and chopped
2 tablespoons olive oil
¼ teaspoon dried oregano leaves
⅛ teaspoon salt
⅛ teaspoon pepper

1 serving

Place capellini in shallow bowl or deep plate. Top with eggplant, green pepper and tomatoes. Drizzle with oil. Sprinkle with oregano, salt and pepper. Cover bowl with plastic wrap. Microwave at High for 5 to 6 minutes, or until capellini is tender, rotating bowl once. Pierce plastic wrap with tip of knife to release steam. Remove wrap. Cover with wax paper or microwave cooking paper. Let stand for 5 minutes. Before serving, toss vegetables gently with capellini.

Per Serving: Calories: 530 • Protein: 11 g. • Carbohydrate: 61 g. • Fat: 29 g. • Cholesterol: 0 • Sodium: 650 mg.
Exchanges: 2 starch, 6 vegetable, 5 fat

Italian Tortellini & Beans

4 oz. uncooked fresh tortellini (1 cup)
1 can (8 oz.) kidney beans or garbanzo beans, rinsed and drained
1 can (8 oz.) tomato sauce
¼ teaspoon Italian seasoning
⅛ teaspoon salt
⅛ teaspoon cayenne
1 tablespoon sliced green onion
1 cup fresh broccoli flowerets

1 serving

In shallow bowl or deep plate, combine tortellini, beans, tomato sauce, Italian seasoning, salt and cayenne. Sprinkle with onion and broccoli. Cover bowl with plastic wrap. Microwave at High for 5 to 6 minutes, or until tortellini is tender, rotating bowl once. Pierce plastic wrap with tip of knife to release steam. Remove wrap. Cover with wax paper or microwave cooking paper. Let stand for 5 minutes. Before serving, toss vegetables gently with tortellini.

Per Serving: Calories: 600 • Protein: 31 g. • Carbohydrate: 115 g. • Fat: 4 g. • Cholesterol: 83 mg. • Sodium: 1700 mg.
Exchanges: 6 starch, 5 vegetable, ½ fat

Winter Fruited French Toast

2 tablespoons margarine or butter

2 tablespoons packed brown sugar

⅛ teaspoon ground cinnamon
Dash ground nutmeg
Dash ground cloves

1 teaspoon lemon juice

½ medium apple, cored and sliced (1 cup)

½ medium pear, cored and sliced (1 cup)

2 slices frozen French toast, cut in half diagonally

1 serving

In medium mixing bowl, microwave margarine at High for 45 seconds to 1 minute, or until melted. Add sugar, cinnamon, nutmeg, cloves and juice. Stir until smooth. Add apple and pear slices. Toss to coat. Place French toast on dinner plate. Top with fruit mixture. Cover plate with plastic wrap. Microwave at High for 4 to 5 minutes, or until fruit is tender, rotating plate once. Pierce plastic wrap with tip of knife to release steam. Remove wrap.

Per Serving: Calories: 640 • Protein: 8 g. • Carbohydrate: 96 g. • Fat: 28 g.
• Cholesterol: N/A • Sodium: 710 mg.
Exchanges: 2 starch, 4 fruit, 5½ fat

Steamed Vegetable Platter ▲
with Garlic Basil Butter

1 medium red onion
8 oz. fresh broccoli, broken into large pieces
8 oz. fresh cauliflower, broken into large pieces
1 cup fresh baby carrots
3 tablespoons margarine or butter
¼ teaspoon dried basil leaves
⅛ teaspoon garlic powder

1 serving

Peel onion and carefully hollow out, leaving ¼-inch shell. Place in center of dinner plate. Arrange broccoli, cauliflower and carrots around onion shell. Place remaining ingredients in onion shell. Cover plate with plastic wrap. Microwave at High for 5 to 6 minutes, or until vegetables are tender-crisp, rotating plate once. Pierce plastic wrap with tip of knife to release steam. Remove wrap. Gently stir margarine mixture in onion shell. To serve, dip vegetables in margarine mixture.

Per Serving: Calories: 520 • Protein: 14 g. • Carbohydrate: 46 g. • Fat: 36 g. • Cholesterol: 0 • Sodium: 540 mg.
Exchanges: 9 vegetable, 7 fat

Steamed Potatoes & Green Bean Platter

8 oz. red potatoes, cut into 1-inch cubes
8 oz. sweet potatoes, peeled and thinly sliced
4 oz. fresh whole green beans
¾ teaspoon grated lemon peel, divided
2 teaspoons water
⅓ cup sour cream
½ teaspoon dried marjoram leaves
Dash sugar

1 serving

Arrange potatoes, sweet potatoes and beans on dinner plate. Sprinkle with ½ teaspoon peel and the water. Cover plate with plastic wrap. Microwave at High for 6 to 7 minutes, or until vegetables are tender, rotating plate once. Pierce plastic wrap with tip of knife to release steam. Remove wrap. In small bowl, combine sour cream, remaining ¼ teaspoon peel, the marjoram and sugar. Serve with warm vegetables.

Per Serving: Calories: 630 • Protein: 13 g. • Carbohydrate: 108 g. • Fat: 18 g. • Cholesterol: 36 mg. • Sodium: 95 mg.
Exchanges: 5 starch, 6 vegetable, 3 fat

American Stir-fry

Shrimp Paella

Use a 2-quart batter bowl and a wooden spoon, which may be left in the bowl during microwaving.

American Stir-fry: Techniques

Reinvent the stir-fry. Americanize the popular Oriental cooking technique, using the microwave oven and combinations of ingredients and seasonings that reflect the diversity of American taste.

These fresh-tasting low-fat recipes microwave quickly in an uncovered 2-quart glass batter bowl. Microwaved stir-fries are even easier than conventional, because there is practically no stirring, and no sticking or scorching means easy cleanup.

Be sure to have all ingredients ready before you begin to cook. Start with longer-cooking foods. When these are partially cooked, stir in items with shorter cooking times, so that each food retains freshness and character.

Each meal is nutritionally complete; if you prefer an even more substantial dish, serve the stir-fry with rice, noodles, couscous or toast.

Leave bowl uncovered during cooking to allow steam to escape.

Serve over a bed of rice or pasta on a family-style platter or on individual plates.

Three Microwave Stir-fry Techniques

Long-cooking vegetables.
Microwave uncooked meats and seafood first. Remove them from bowl while cooking vegetables.

Precooked meats. Microwave vegetables until nearly done before adding meat.

Short-cooking vegetables.
Microwave meat or poultry, then stir in quick-cooking vegetables.

Santa Fe Pepper Steak

¼ cup fresh lime juice
2 tablespoons vegetable oil
2 cloves garlic, minced
½ teaspoon cayenne
1-lb. boneless beef sirloin steak, about ½ inch thick, cut into ¼-inch strips
3 cups green, red and yellow pepper strips (2 × ¼-inch strips)
1 can (6 oz.) tomato paste
1 cup seeded chopped tomato
½ cup sliced green onions
1 can (4 oz.) chopped green chilies, drained
1 cup frozen corn
1 tablespoon snipped fresh parsley
½ teaspoon salt
1 cup chopped avocado (optional)

4 servings

In 2-quart batter bowl, combine juice, oil, garlic, cayenne and beef. Marinate at room temperature for 15 minutes. Microwave at High for 4 to 7 minutes, or until meat is no longer pink, stirring twice. Remove meat from bowl with slotted spoon. Set aside. In same batter bowl, stir pepper strips into reserved marinade.

Microwave at High for 4 to 5 minutes, or until tender-crisp, stirring once. Stir in tomato paste. Mix well. Stir in remaining ingredients, except beef and avocado. Microwave at High for 4 to 5 minutes, or until hot, stirring once. Stir in beef. Microwave at High for 1 to 2 minutes, or until hot. Serve over hot cooked rice or in soft or hard tortilla shells, if desired. Sprinkle with avocado.

Per Serving: Calories: 330 • Protein: 27 g.
• Carbohydrate: 28 g. • Fat: 13 g.
• Cholesterol: 66 mg. • Sodium: 660 mg.
Exchanges: 1 starch, 2½ lean meat,
2½ vegetable, 1 fat

Corned Beef & Cabbage

  5 small new potatoes, quartered (about 8 oz.)
  ½ cup sliced red onion
  2 tablespoons vegetable oil
  1 teaspoon caraway seed
  ½ teaspoon salt
  1 cup diagonally sliced carrots
  2 cups shredded cabbage (½-inch slices)
  1 pkg. (2.5 oz.) thinly sliced fully cooked lean
      corned beef, cut into 2 × ½-inch strips
  2 tablespoons horseradish sauce

4 servings

In 2-quart batter bowl, combine potatoes, onion, oil, caraway seed and salt. Microwave at High for 5 minutes, stirring once. Stir in carrots. Microwave at High for 2 to 4 minutes, or until carrots are tender-crisp. Stir in cabbage. Microwave at High for 4 to 6 minutes, or until vegetables are tender, stirring once. Add corned beef and horseradish sauce. Mix well. Microwave at High for 1 to 2 minutes, or until hot.

Per Serving: Calories: 180 • Protein: 6 g. • Carbohydrate: 17 g.
• Fat: 10 g. • Cholesterol: 17 mg. • Sodium: 500 mg.
Exchanges: ½ starch, ½ high-fat meat, 2 vegetable, 1 fat

Roast Beef Hash ▲

  2 tablespoons margarine or butter
  2 cups cubed red potatoes (1-inch cubes)
1½ cups frozen mixed vegetables
  ⅓ cup sliced green onions
  1 tablespoon Worcestershire sauce
  ½ teaspoon dried basil leaves
  ¼ teaspoon salt
  ⅛ teaspoon pepper
1- lb. fully cooked roast beef, cut into thin
      strips

4 servings

In 2-quart batter bowl, microwave margarine at High for 45 seconds to 1 minute, or until melted. Stir in potatoes. Microwave at High for 4 to 5 minutes, or until potatoes are tender-crisp, stirring once. Stir in mixed vegetables, onions, Worcestershire sauce, basil, salt and pepper. Mix well. Microwave at High for 2 to 4 minutes, or until vegetables are tender, stirring once. Stir in beef. Microwave at High for 3 to 4 minutes, or until hot, stirring once.

Per Serving: Calories: 390 • Protein: 39 g. • Carbohydrate: 22 g.
• Fat: 15 g. • Cholesterol: 109 mg. • Sodium: 330 mg.
Exchanges: 1½ starch, 4½ lean meat, ½ fat

◄ Honey Barbecue Pork

2 tablespoons margarine or
   butter, divided
1‑lb. pork tenderloin, sliced
   (½‑inch slices)
2 teaspoons cornstarch
3 tablespoons honey
2 tablespoons lemon juice
1 teaspoon liquid smoke
   flavoring
½ teaspoon salt
¼ teaspoon garlic powder
¼ teaspoon pepper
5 small new potatoes,
   quartered (about 8 oz.)
1 medium onion, thinly sliced
2 medium carrots, cut into
   1‑inch lengths
1 medium green pepper, cut
   into 1‑inch chunks (1 cup)

4 servings

In 2‑quart batter bowl, microwave 1 tablespoon margarine at
High for 45 seconds to 1 minute,
or until melted. Stir in pork. Microwave at High for 6 to 7 minutes,
or until meat is no longer pink,
stirring twice. Drain. Remove
meat from bowl. Set aside.

Place cornstarch in small mixing
bowl. Blend in honey, juice, liquid smoke, salt, garlic powder
and pepper. In same batter bowl,
microwave remaining 1 tablespoon margarine at High for 45
seconds to 1 minute, or until
melted. Stir in honey mixture,
potatoes, onion and carrots.

Microwave at High for 10 to 14
minutes, or until vegetables are
tender, stirring 3 times. Stir in
green peppers. Microwave at
High for 1 to 3 minutes, or until
green peppers are tender-crisp,
stirring once. Stir in pork. Microwave at High for 1 to 2 minutes,
or until hot.

Per Serving: Calories: 350 • Protein: 28 g.
• Carbohydrate: 36 g. • Fat: 10 g.
• Cholesterol: 83 mg. • Sodium: 410 mg.
Exchanges: 1 starch, 3 lean meat,
2½ vegetable, ½ fruit, ½ fat

Two Potato & Sausage Combo

2 cups frozen potato nuggets
2 tablespoons margarine or
   butter
½ teaspoon seasoned salt
¼ teaspoon garlic powder
5 small new potatoes, cut into
   1‑inch chunks (about 8 oz.)

1 medium onion, thinly sliced
1 cup chopped green pepper
1‑lb. fully cooked Polish
   sausage, cut in half
   lengthwise and then into
   2‑inch pieces

4 servings

Bake potato nuggets as directed on package. In 2‑quart batter bowl,
microwave margarine at High for 45 seconds to 1 minute, or until
melted. Stir in salt, garlic powder and new potatoes. Microwave at
High for 8 to 10 minutes, or until potatoes are tender, stirring twice.
Stir in onion and green pepper. Microwave at High for 4 to 5 minutes,
or until vegetables are tender. Stir in sausage. Microwave at High
for 5 to 6 minutes, or until hot. Stir in potato nuggets.

Per Serving: Calories: 540 • Protein: 19 g. • Carbohydrate: 28 g. • Fat: 39 g.
• Cholesterol: 79 mg. • Sodium: 1280 mg.
Exchanges: 1½ starch, 2 high-fat meat, 1 vegetable, 4½ fat

Citrus Ham Toss

 2 tablespoons margarine or
   butter
 1 tablespoon cornstarch
 ½ teaspoon salt
 ¼ teaspoon cayenne
 ¾ cup orange juice
 ½ medium yellow pepper, cut
   into 1-inch chunks
 ½ medium red pepper, cut
   into 1-inch chunks
 ½ medium green pepper, cut
   into 1-inch chunks
 1-lb. fully cooked ham, cut
   into strips (1½ × ¼-inch
   strips)
 1 cup halved cherry tomatoes
 ½ cup sliced green onions
 2 tablespoons snipped fresh
   chives

4 servings

In 2-quart batter bowl, microwave margarine at High for 45 seconds to 1 minute, or until melted. Stir in cornstarch, salt and cayenne. Blend in juice. Microwave at High for 3 to 5 minutes, or until mixture is thickened and translucent, stirring 3 times. Stir in pepper chunks. Microwave at High for 2 to 4 minutes, or until peppers are tender-crisp, stirring once. Stir in remaining ingredients. Microwave at High for 4 to 5 minutes, or until hot, stirring once.

Per Serving: Calories: 260 • Protein: 25 g.• Carbohydrate: 13 g. • Fat: 12 g.
• Cholesterol: 60 mg. • Sodium: 1700 mg.
Exchanges: 3½ lean meat, 1 vegetable, ½ fruit, ½ fat

Pineapple Pork & Peppers

- 2 teaspoons cornstarch
- ¼ teaspoon ground ginger
- ¼ teaspoon crushed red pepper flakes
- 2 tablespoons soy sauce
- 1 tablespoon vegetable oil
- 1-lb. boneless pork loin, cut into 2-inch strips
- 1 can (8 oz.) pineapple chunks in juice, drained (reserve 2 tablespoons juice)
- 1 cup red pepper chunks (1-inch chunks)
- 1 cup green pepper chunks (1-inch chunks)

4 servings

In 2-quart batter bowl, combine cornstarch, ginger, red pepper flakes, soy sauce and oil. Add pork. Toss to coat. Marinate at room temperature for 5 minutes. Stir in reserved juice. Microwave at High for 6 to 8 minutes, or until meat is no longer pink, stirring twice.

Stir in pepper chunks. Microwave at High for 4 to 5 minutes, or until peppers are tender-crisp, stirring once. Stir in pineapple chunks. Microwave at High for 2 to 3 minutes, or until hot.

Per Serving: Calories: 290 • Protein: 25 g. • Carbohydrate: 11 g. • Fat: 16 g.
• Cholesterol: 81 mg. • Sodium: 580 mg.
Exchanges: 3 lean meat, ½ vegetable, ½ fruit, 1½ fat

Tex-Mex Pork & Beans ▶

 2 teaspoons cornstarch
½ teaspoon chili powder
¼ teaspoon salt
¼ teaspoon sugar
¼ teaspoon ground cumin
⅛ teaspoon cayenne
1- lb. pork tenderloin,
     sliced (¼-inch slices)
 1 can (14½ oz.) diced
     tomatoes, drained
½ cup sliced red onion
 1 cup frozen corn
 1 medium zucchini, cut into
     1½-inch strips
 1 can (15½ oz.) black beans,
     rinsed and drained

4 servings

In 2-quart batter bowl, combine
cornstarch, chili powder, salt,
sugar, cumin and cayenne. Add
pork. Toss to coat. Stir in tomatoes and onion. Microwave at
High for 6 to 9 minutes, or until
meat is no longer pink, stirring
twice. Stir in corn and zucchini.
Microwave at High for 5 to 6 minutes, or until vegetables are
tender, stirring once. Stir in beans.
Microwave at High for 2 to 3 minutes, or until hot.

Per Serving: Calories: 320 • Protein: 35 g.
• Carbohydrate: 34 g. • Fat: 6 g.
• Cholesterol: 83 mg. • Sodium: 210 mg.
Exchanges: 1½ starch, 3 lean meat,
2½ vegetable

Dijon Ham & Apples

 2 tablespoons margarine or
     butter
 2 cups halved fresh Brussels
     sprouts
 2 tablespoons Dijon mustard
 2 tablespoons maple syrup
1- lb. fully cooked ham, cut
     into julienne strips
     (2 × ¼-inch strips)
 1 medium Rome apple, cored
     and thinly sliced

4 servings

In 2-quart batter bowl, microwave margarine at High for 45 seconds
to 1 minute, or until melted. Stir in Brussels sprouts. Microwave at
High for 5 to 6 minutes, or until tender-crisp, stirring once. Stir in mustard, maple syrup and ham. Microwave at High for 2 to 3 minutes,
or until hot, stirring once. Stir in apple slices.

Per Serving: Calories: 290 • Protein: 26 g. • Carbohydrate: 20 g. • Fat: 13 g.
• Cholesterol: 60 mg. • Sodium: 1540 mg.
Exchanges: 3½ lean meat, 1 vegetable, 1 fruit, ½ fat

Hot & Sour Chicken

- 2 boneless whole chicken breasts (8 to 10 oz. each), split in half, skin removed, cut into 1-inch pieces
- 2 tablespoons soy sauce, divided
- 1 teaspoon sesame oil, divided
- 1 cup ready-to-serve chicken broth
- 1 tablespoon cornstarch
- 1 tablespoon vinegar
- 1/4 teaspoon red pepper sauce
- 1/4 teaspoon white pepper
- 2 cups shredded Chinese cabbage (Napa)
- 1 cup shredded carrots
- 6 green onions, cut into 1-inch lengths
- 1 can (8 oz.) sliced water chestnuts, rinsed and drained
- 1 can (8 oz.) bamboo shoots, rinsed and drained

4 servings

In 2-quart batter bowl, combine chicken, 1 tablespoon soy sauce and 1/2 teaspoon oil. Microwave at High for 5 to 7 minutes, or until meat is no longer pink, stirring twice. Drain. Remove meat from bowl. Set aside. In same bowl, combine broth, cornstarch, vinegar, remaining 1 tablespoon soy sauce and 1/2 teaspoon oil, the red pepper sauce and pepper.

Microwave at High for 4 to 5 minutes, or until mixture is thickened and translucent, stirring 2 or 3 times. Stir in cabbage, carrots and onions. Microwave at High for 1 to 2 minutes, or until vegetables are tender-crisp. Stir in chicken, water chestnuts and bamboo shoots. Microwave at High for 1 to 2 minutes, or until hot.

Per Serving: Calories: 230 • Protein: 28 g.
• Carbohydrate: 18 g. • Fat: 5 g.
• Cholesterol: 67 mg. • Sodium: 810 mg.
Exchanges: 3 lean meat, 3½ vegetable

Summer Italian Chicken

2　boneless whole chicken breasts (8 to 10 oz. each), split in half, skin removed, cut into 1-inch pieces
½　cup Italian dressing
½　teaspoon dried basil leaves
½　teaspoon dried marjoram leaves
2　cups fresh cauliflowerets
1　cup julienne carrots (2 × ¼-inch strips)
1　cup julienne zucchini (2 × ¼-inch strips)
½　cup sliced celery

4 servings

In 2-quart batter bowl, combine chicken, dressing, basil and marjoram. Marinate at room temperature for 15 minutes. Microwave at High for 6 to 8 minutes, or until meat is no longer pink, stirring twice. Remove meat from bowl with slotted spoon. Set aside. Stir cauliflower and carrots into reserved marinade. Microwave at High for 4 to 5 minutes, or until tender-crisp, stirring once. Stir in zucchini and celery. Microwave at High for 4 to 5 minutes, or until tender-crisp, stirring once. Stir in chicken. Microwave at High for 2 to 3 minutes, or until hot.

Per Serving: Calories: 300 • Protein: 26 g. • Carbohydrate: 10 g.
• Fat: 17 g. • Cholesterol: 67 mg. • Sodium: 320 mg.
Exchanges: 3 lean meat, 2 vegetable, 2 fat

Dilled Chicken & Spring Vegetables ▲

2　boneless whole chicken breasts (8 to 10 oz. each), split in half, skin removed, cut into ½-inch strips
1　teaspoon dried dill weed, divided
1　pkg. (9 oz.) frozen peas
¼　cup sliced green onions
½　cup sour cream
½　teaspoon salt
4　cups torn fresh spinach leaves
1　cup quartered cherry tomatoes

4 servings

In 2-quart batter bowl, combine chicken and ½ teaspoon dill weed. Microwave at High for 4 to 6 minutes, or until meat is no longer pink, stirring twice. Drain. Remove meat from bowl. Set aside. In same bowl, combine peas and onions. Microwave at High for 5 to 6 minutes, or until tender-crisp, stirring once. Stir in chicken, remaining ½ teaspoon dill weed, the sour cream and salt. Microwave at High for 2 to 3 minutes, or until hot. Stir in spinach. Microwave at High for 1 to 2 minutes, or until spinach begins to wilt. Stir in tomatoes.

Per Serving: Calories: 260 • Protein: 31 g. • Carbohydrate: 14 g.
• Fat: 10 g. • Cholesterol: 80 mg. • Sodium: 460 mg.
Exchanges: ½ starch, 3 lean meat, 1½ vegetable, ½ fat

Chicken & Two Pepper Curry

2 boneless whole chicken
   breasts (8 to 10 oz. each),
   split in half, skin removed,
   cut into 2-inch strips
1 tablespoon all-purpose flour
2 tablespoons olive oil
2 tablespoons curry powder
½ teaspoon salt
1 cup chopped onions
1 cup celery chunks (1-inch
   chunks)
1 cup green pepper strips
   (2 × ¼-inch strips)
1 cup red pepper strips
   (2 × ¼-inch strips)
1 medium tomato, cut into
   wedges
¼ cup raisins

        4 servings

In large plastic food-storage bag, place chicken and flour. Shake to coat. Set aside. In 2-quart batter bowl, combine oil, curry powder and salt. Stir in chicken. Microwave at High for 5 to 8 minutes, or until meat is no longer pink, stirring 2 or 3 times. Stir in onions and celery. Microwave at High for 4 to 5 minutes, or until vegetables are tender-crisp, stirring once. Stir in pepper strips. Microwave at High for 3 to 4 minutes, or until peppers are tender-crisp, stirring once. Stir in tomato wedges. Microwave at High for 1 to 2 minutes, or until hot. Top each serving evenly with raisins.

Per Serving: Calories: 270 • Protein: 27 g. • Carbohydrate: 20 g. • Fat: 10 g.
• Cholesterol: 67 mg. • Sodium: 360 mg.
Exchanges: 3 lean meat, 2½ vegetable, ½ fruit, ½ fat

Southern-style Chicken

3 slices bacon, cut into
   1-inch pieces
2 boneless whole chicken
   breasts (8 to 10 oz. each),
   split in half, skin removed,
   cut into 2-inch strips
½ teaspoon dried thyme
   leaves
¼ teaspoon garlic powder
⅛ teaspoon cayenne
1 can (15¾ oz.) black-eyed
   peas, rinsed and drained
1 jar (2 oz.) sliced pimiento,
   drained
1 can (15 oz.) baby corn on
   the cob, rinsed and
   drained, cut into 1-inch
   pieces
2 cups torn fresh spinach
   leaves

4 servings

In 2-quart batter bowl, microwave bacon at High for 4 to 6 minutes, or until brown and crisp, stirring twice. Add chicken, thyme, garlic powder and cayenne. Mix well. Microwave at High for 4 to 6 minutes, or until meat is no longer pink, stirring once or twice. Stir in peas, pimiento and corn. Microwave at High for 3 to 4 minutes, or until vegetables are hot, stirring once. Stir in spinach. Microwave at High for 1 to 1½ minutes, or until spinach is wilted.

Per Serving: Calories: 260 • Protein: 33 g. • Carbohydrate: 18 g. • Fat: 6 g.
• Cholesterol: 71 mg. • Sodium: 290 mg.
Exchanges: 1 starch, 3 lean meat, ½ vegetable

Chicken, Prunes & Apricots Mélange

2 boneless whole chicken breasts (8 to 10 oz. each), split in half, skin removed, cut into 1-inch pieces
1 cup pitted prunes
1 cup dried apricot halves
2 tablespoons olive oil
1 clove garlic, minced
½ teaspoon dried thyme leaves
1 tablespoon cornstarch
½ teaspoon pepper
¼ cup ready-to-serve chicken broth
¼ cup white wine
2 tablespoons red wine vinegar
2 teaspoons Dijon mustard

4 servings

In 2-quart batter bowl, combine chicken, prunes, apricots, oil, garlic and thyme. Microwave at High for 6 to 9 minutes, or until meat is no longer pink, stirring 2 or 3 times. Set aside.

In 1-cup measure, combine cornstarch and pepper. Blend in remaining ingredients. Add to chicken mixture. Mix well. Microwave at High for 4 to 5 minutes, or until sauce is thickened and translucent, stirring once.

Per Serving: Calories: 390 • Protein: 27 g.
• Carbohydrate: 48 g. • Fat: 10 g.
• Cholesterol: 67 mg. • Sodium: 140 mg.
Exchanges: 3 lean meat, 3 fruit

Turkey & Stuffing

1 lb. uncooked turkey breast slices, cut crosswise into ½-inch strips
2 tablespoons margarine or butter
8 oz. quartered fresh mushrooms (2 cups)
1 cup sliced celery (1-inch slices)
½ cup chopped onion
½ teaspoon salt
¼ teaspoon ground sage
¼ teaspoon pepper
2 cups herb-seasoned stuffing cubes
1 medium Rome apple, cored, cut in half crosswise and sliced
¾ cup ready-to-serve chicken broth
½ cup chopped pecans

4 servings

In 2-quart batter bowl, micro-wave turkey at High for 5 to 6 minutes, or until no longer pink, stirring twice. Drain. Remove meat from bowl. Set aside. In same batter bowl, microwave margarine at High for 45 seconds to 1 minute, or until melted. Stir in mushrooms, celery, onion, salt, sage and pepper.

Microwave at High for 4 to 5 minutes, or until vegetables are tender, stirring twice. Stir in stuffing cubes, apple and broth. Microwave at High for 4 to 5 minutes, or until mixture is hot and liquid is absorbed, stirring once. Stir in turkey and pecans. Microwave at High for 1 to 2 minutes, or until hot.

Per Serving: Calories: 390 • Protein: 32 g.
• Carbohydrate: 28 g. • Fat: 17 g.
• Cholesterol: 71 mg. • Sodium: 810 mg.
Exchanges: 1 starch, 3½ lean meat, 1 vegetable, ½ fruit

Pesto Chicken ▲

2 boneless whole chicken breasts (8 to 10 oz. each), split in half, skin removed
¼ cup pesto
8 oz. fresh asparagus spears, cut into 1½-inch lengths

1 medium yellow summer squash, sliced (1 cup)
1 cup halved cherry tomatoes
4 teaspoons pine nuts

4 servings

Cut each chicken breast half into 4 pieces. In 2-quart batter bowl, combine chicken and pesto. Toss to coat. Marinate at room temperature for 5 minutes. Microwave at High for 6 to 7 minutes, or until meat is no longer pink, stirring twice. Stir in asparagus. Microwave at High for 2 minutes. Stir in squash. Microwave at High for 3 to 4 minutes, or until vegetables are tender-crisp, stirring once. Stir in tomatoes. Sprinkle each serving with 1 teaspoon pine nuts.

Per Serving: Calories: 240 • Protein: 28 g. • Carbohydrate: 6 g. • Fat: 12 g.
• Cholesterol: 68 mg. • Sodium: 95 mg.
Exchanges: 3½ lean meat, 1 vegetable, ½ fat

Shrimp Paella

1 lb. large shrimp, shelled
   and deveined
2 tablespoons olive oil
2 cloves garlic, minced
1 teaspoon dried rosemary
   leaves, crushed
½ teaspoon crushed red
   pepper flakes
½ teaspoon salt
   Pinch saffron
   Ready-to-serve chicken broth
1 tablespoon cornstarch
1 medium green pepper,
   cut into 1-inch chunks
½ cup coarsely chopped red
   onion
1 medium tomato, cut into
   8 wedges
½ cup sliced black olives

4 servings

With sharp knife, carefully cut down middle of back of each shrimp without cutting all the way through. Set aside. In 2-quart batter bowl, combine oil, garlic, rosemary, red pepper flakes, salt and saffron. Stir in shrimp. Microwave at 70% (Medium High) for 6 to 8 minutes, or until shrimp are firm and opaque, stirring twice. Remove shrimp from bowl with slotted spoon. Set aside.

Add broth to reserved liquid in bowl to yield 1 cup. Blend in cornstarch. Stir in green pepper and onion. Microwave at High for 8 to 10 minutes, or until vegetables are tender-crisp and mixture is thickened and translucent, stirring every 2 minutes. Stir in shrimp, tomato and olives.

Per Serving: Calories: 230 • Protein: 25 g.
• Carbohydrate: 8 g. • Fat: 10 g.
• Cholesterol: 221 mg. • Sodium: 770 mg.
Exchanges: 3 lean meat, 1½ vegetable,
1 fat

Coconut Shrimp ▲

½ cup flaked coconut
1 lb. medium shrimp, shelled
   and deveined
2 teaspoons cornstarch
¼ cup cream of coconut
¼ cup water
3 tablespoons lime juice

1 cup fresh pea pods
½ fresh pineapple, peeled
   and cut into 1-inch chunks
   (2½ cups)
2 medium oranges, peeled
   and chopped (2 cups)

4 servings

Heat conventional oven to 325°F. Sprinkle coconut in even layer on baking sheet. Bake for 5 to 6 minutes, or until light brown and toasted, stirring twice. Set aside. In 2-quart batter bowl, microwave shrimp at 70% (Medium High) for 5 to 7 minutes, or until firm and opaque, stirring twice. Drain. Remove shrimp from bowl. Set aside. Place cornstarch in same batter bowl. Blend in cream of coconut, water and juice. Microwave at High for 3 to 4 minutes, or until hot, stirring once. Stir in shrimp and pea pods. Microwave at High for 1 to 2 minutes, or until hot. Stir in pineapple and oranges. Sprinkle with toasted coconut.

Per Serving: Calories: 320 • Protein: 27 g. • Carbohydrate: 29 g. • Fat: 12 g.
• Cholesterol: 221 mg. • Sodium: 270 mg.
Exchanges: 1 starch, 3½ lean meat, 1 fruit, ½ fat

Dilled Salmon & Spring Vegetables

1 lb. salmon fillets, skin removed, cut into 1-inch pieces
2 medium carrots
1 small yellow summer squash (about 4 oz.)
1 lb. fresh asparagus spears, cut into 1½-inch lengths (2 cups)
¼ cup plus 2 tablespoons olive oil, divided
1 tablespoon lemon juice
1½ teaspoons Dijon mustard
½ teaspoon dried dill weed
¼ teaspoon salt
¼ teaspoon sugar

4 servings

In 2-quart batter bowl, microwave salmon at 70% (Medium High) for 6 to 7 minutes, or until fish flakes easily with fork, gently re-arranging pieces twice. Drain. Remove fish from bowl. Set aside.

Using vegetable peeler, cut lengthwise ribbons from carrots and squash, discarding center portion of vegetables. In same batter bowl, combine vegetable ribbons, asparagus and 2 table-spoons oil. Microwave at High for 3 to 5 minutes, or until aspar-agus is tender, stirring once.

In 1-cup measure, combine re-maining ¼ cup oil, the juice, mustard, dill weed, salt and sugar. Add salmon and oil mix-ture to vegetables. Toss gently to coat.

Per Serving: Calories: 390 • Protein: 27 g.
• Carbohydrate: 9 g. • Fat: 28 g.
• Cholesterol: 62 mg. • Sodium: 220 mg.
Exchanges: 3 lean meat, 2 vegetable, 3½ fat

Scallop Salad ▲

2 tablespoons olive oil
½ teaspoon crushed red pepper flakes
1 lb. bay scallops
Ready-to-serve chicken broth
1 tablespoon cornstarch

1 cup julienne carrots (2 × ⅛-inch strips)
1 medium cucumber, cut in half lengthwise and thinly sliced (2 cups)
½ cup julienne radishes (1 × ⅛-inch strips)
2 cups shredded leaf lettuce

4 servings

In 2-quart batter bowl, combine oil and red pepper flakes. Stir in scallops. Microwave at 70% (Medium High) for 5 to 6 minutes, or until scallops are firm and opaque, stirring twice. Remove scallops from bowl with slotted spoon. Set aside. Add broth to reserved liquid in bowl to yield 1 cup. Blend in cornstarch. Stir in carrots. Microwave at High for 8 to 9 minutes, or until carrots are tender and mixture is thickened and translucent, stirring twice. Stir in scallops and remaining ingredients. Microwave at High for 1 to 2 minutes, or until hot.

Per Serving: Calories: 200 • Protein: 21 g. • Carbohydrate: 11 g. • Fat: 8 g.
• Cholesterol: 37 mg. • Sodium: 300 mg.
Exchanges: 2½ lean meat, 2 vegetable, ½ fat

Spicy Moroccan Vegetables ▲

2　tablespoons olive oil
2　cloves garlic, minced
1　teaspoon ground cumin
½　teaspoon salt
¼　teaspoon freshly ground black pepper
1　cup chopped onions
1　cup peeled diced turnip (¼-inch cubes)
1　cup thinly sliced carrots
1　cup red pepper chunks (1-inch chunks)
1　cup thinly sliced zucchini
1　can (16 oz.) garbanzo beans, rinsed and
　　drained
1　cup raisins
3　tablespoons snipped fresh parsley

4 servings

In 2-quart batter bowl, combine oil, garlic, cumin, salt, pepper, onions, turnip and carrots. Microwave at High for 8 to 9 minutes, or until vegetables are tender, stirring 2 or 3 times. Stir in red pepper and zucchini. Microwave at High for 3 to 4 minutes, or until tender-crisp, stirring once. Stir in garbanzo beans, raisins and parsley. Microwave at High for 2 to 3 minutes, or until hot, stirring once.

Per Serving: Calories: 340 • Protein: 9 g. • Carbohydrate: 60 g. • Fat: 9 g. • Cholesterol: 0 • Sodium: 320 mg.
Exchanges: 2 starch, 3 vegetable, 1 fruit, 1½ fat

Fiesta Egg Scramble

1　tablespoon margarine or butter
⅓　cup chopped red pepper
¼　cup sliced green onions
2　tablespoons canned chopped green
　　chilies, drained
6　eggs, beaten
½　cup shredded Monterey Jack cheese
¼　cup milk
　　Tortilla chips (optional)
　　Salsa (optional)
　　Avocado slices (optional)

4 servings

In 2-quart batter bowl, microwave margarine at High for 45 seconds to 1 minute, or until melted. Stir in red pepper, onions and chilies. Microwave at High for 2 to 3 minutes, or until vegetables are tender, stirring once. Stir in eggs, cheese and milk. Blend with whisk. Microwave at High for 4 to 7 minutes, or until egg mixture is set but still moist, stirring after 2 minutes and then every minute to break up cooked portions. Serve on bed of tortilla chips, topped with salsa and garnished with avocado slices.

Per Serving: Calories: 200 • Protein: 14 g. • Carbohydrate: 3 g. • Fat: 15 g. • Cholesterol: 334 mg. • Sodium: 210 mg.
Exchanges: 2 medium-fat meat, ½ vegetable, 1 fat

Ratatouille with Potatoes

- 2 tablespoons olive oil
- 2 cloves garlic, minced
- ½ teaspoon dried basil leaves
- ½ teaspoon dried thyme leaves
- ½ teaspoon dried oregano leaves
- ½ teaspoon salt
- ¼ teaspoon pepper
- 5 small new potatoes, cut into ¾-inch chunks (about 8 oz.)
- 1 small eggplant (about 10 oz.), cut into 1-inch chunks
- 8 oz. fresh mushrooms, sliced (2 cups)
- 1 medium zucchini, thinly sliced (1 cup)
- ½ cup chopped red onion
- 1 medium green pepper, cut into 1-inch chunks
- 3 Roma tomatoes, cut into 1-inch chunks
- ¼ cup freshly grated Parmesan cheese

4 servings

In 2-quart batter bowl, combine oil, garlic, basil, thyme, oregano, salt and pepper. Stir in potatoes and eggplant. Microwave at High for 13 to 15 minutes, or until vegetables are tender-crisp, stirring 2 or 3 times.

Stir in mushrooms, zucchini and onion. Microwave at High for 4 to 5 minutes, or until vegetables are tender-crisp, stirring once. Stir in green pepper and tomatoes. Microwave at High for 4 to 5 minutes, or until vegetables are tender, stirring once. Sprinkle each serving evenly with cheese.

Per Serving: Calories: 200 • Protein: 7 g.
• Carbohydrate: 26 g. • Fat: 9 g.
• Cholesterol: 5 mg. • Sodium: 400 mg.
Exchanges: 1 starch, 2 vegetable, ½ fat

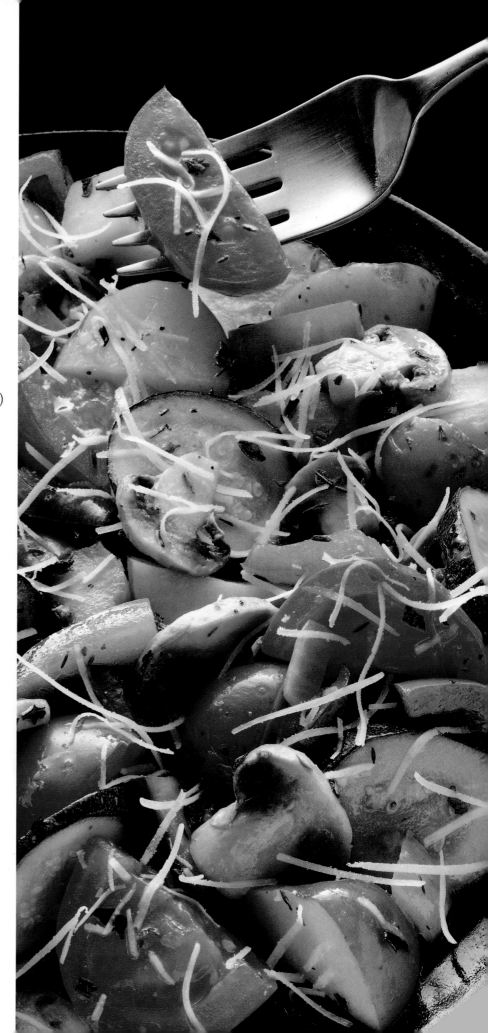

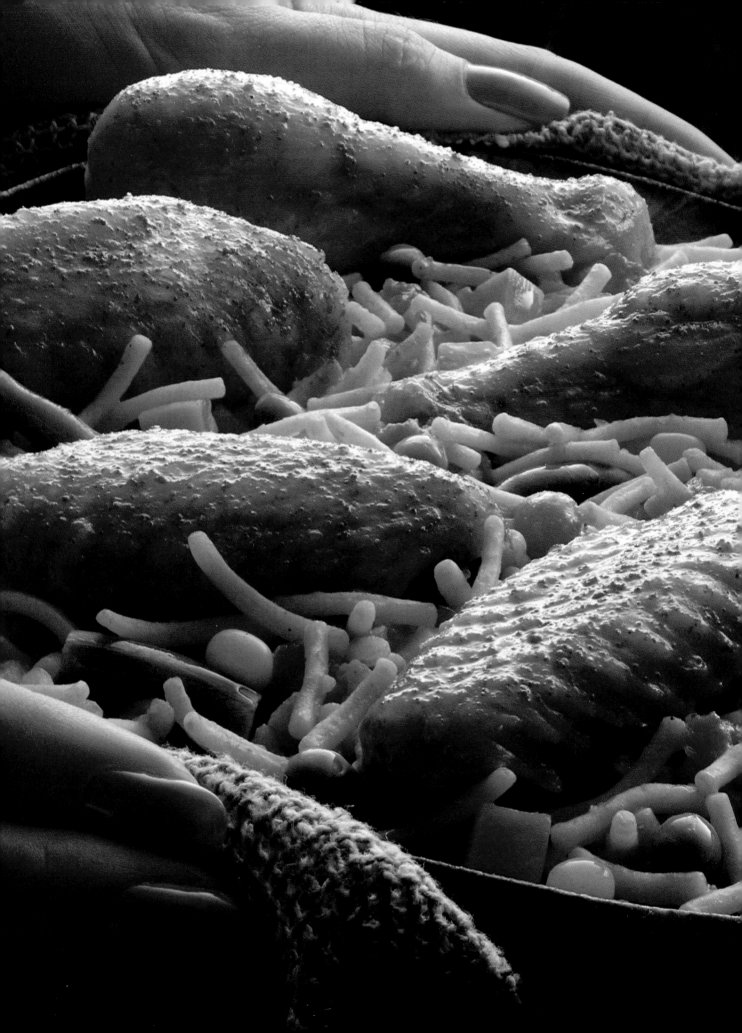

Casseroles

Speedy Spanish Paella

Casseroles: Techniques

Chances are, when you think of one-dish meals, the first thing that comes to mind is a casserole. A mainstay of potluck suppers as well as of the family table, the casserole has its roots in every country represented in the American melting pot. This one-dish meal derives its name from the pot in which it is cooked and served.

A variety of containers can serve as casseroles. The traditional casserole is either round, square or oval with deep sides and a cover. It may be made of oven glass, earthenware, porcelain, Pyroceram™ or enameled cast iron. Some recipes call for baking dishes. These square, rectangular or oval dishes have shallower sides and more cooking surface than a standard casserole. Other suitable containers are soufflé dishes, deep-dish pie plates and earthenware or porcelain vegetable dishes.

The size and shape of the container affects cooking. If a dish is too small, food may boil over. In an overly large dish, food may dry out. If you do not use the container specified in the recipe, be sure to substitute one of similar depth and volume.

If a baking dish or pie plate does not have its dimensions marked on the bottom, measure with a ruler from rim to rim. If necessary, determine the capacity of a casserole by filling it to the top with measured water.

Presentation

Use your imagination to dress up a casserole for presentation at the table. A pretty garnish adds both eye and appetite appeal. One of the simplest ways to style a meal is to use an ornamental earthenware or porcelain casserole or a serving bowl from your dinnerware. Make sure these are microwave or conventional oven-safe and similar to the container called for in the recipe. Give a festive appearance to baking dishes by placing them in baskets, or wrap a dish in a decorative tea towel.

Three Ways to Wrap a Casserole

Center a 2-quart casserole on towel. On each short side, knot corners of towel together snugly to enclose dish.

Secure corners of towel with napkin rings at each end of a rectangular baking dish.

Fold towel in half diagonally. Fold again to fit height of soufflé dish. Wrap around dish; twist ends together and tuck under.

Decorative Garnishes for Casseroles

Sprinkle baked casseroles with herb sprigs, chopped tomato, peppers, red onion or scallions for a fresh, colorful garnish. For additional suggestions, see Soup Toppers, page 110.

Top casseroles with cheese or sliced olives for richer flavor. Canned French-fried onions, croutons or crushed crackers, added during last one-third of cooking time, provide a crisp finish.

Healthy Classic Casseroles: Techniques

Most of us have fond memories of the casseroles "Mother used to make" — hot and homey, rich with creamy sauce or crusty with cheese. It's hard to reconcile those old-fashioned favorites with today's concern for light and healthy nutrition. If only we could have the taste of the past without the calories, fat and sodium.

The recipes in this section evoke nostalgia — Mac and Cheese, Beef Stroganoff, Tuna-Noodle — but they've been modernized to make use of "lighter" ingredients, such as leaner cuts of meat, egg whites or Egg Beaters®, low-fat sour cream and cheeses.

Update Extras

The basic recipes are as close to the traditional dishes as possible. The Update Extras suggest additions that satisfy today's preference for fresh, crisp-textured vegetables.

Reduce sodium by using low-sodium tomatoes and bouillon granules or reduced-sodium soy sauce and soups. Whenever possible, rinse and drain canned foods to reduce sodium further.

Lower the fat content with lean meats, skinned chicken, water-packed canned foods, reduced-calorie mayonnaise and salad dressings, non-fat yogurt, skim milk, evaporated skim milk and nonstick vegetable cooking spray.

Casserole Comparison

The following chart lists each Healthy Classic Casserole and compares per-serving calories, fat and sodium in the traditional recipes with the new, healthy versions. In some cases, fewer calories are derived from fat although total calories remain comparable.

Recipe Title	Calories		Fat (g.)		Sodium (mg.)	
	New	Traditional	New	Traditional	New	Traditional
Stroganoff with a Light Difference vs. Beef Stroganoff	280	490	6	35	500	590
New American Classic Mac & Cheese vs. Macaroni & Cheese	260	380	6	19	370	690
Tomato & Pesto Sauced Spinach Manicotti vs. Spinach-stuffed Manicotti	270	550	4	22	820	1560
Light & Healthy Turkey Tetrazzini vs. Turkey Tetrazzini	280	530	5	31	320	460
New Classics Chicken & Rice vs. Chicken & Rice Casserole	300	410	7	12	350	860
Hamburger & Wild Rice vs. Ground Beef & Wild Rice Casserole	370	370	15	23	320	1210
Lighten-up Tuna-Noodle vs. Tuna-Noodle Casserole	380	300	4	9	570	960
Trimmed-down Taco Bake vs. Taco Bake	370	720	14	43	720	2340
Grandma's Meatless Goulash vs. Goulash	250	470	3	26	300	1310
Enlightened Quiche vs. Quiche Lorraine	260	300	12	19	290	410
Chicken à la King Casserole vs. Chicken à la King	260	490	5	28	530	1250
Lean Vegetable Lasagna vs. Lasagna	260	420	5	19	280	1130
Lean Meat Lasagna vs. Lasagna	340	420	11	19	620	1130

New-fashioned Condensed Soups for Old-fashioned Favorites

Many classic casseroles call for condensed cream soup as a sauce base. For healthy updated versions of family favorites, make your own soup mix from the recipe opposite, and keep it on hand. Store it on a pantry shelf in an airtight container. When reconstituted, it can be used in any recipe that calls for a can of condensed cream soup.

New-fashioned Cream Soups reduce fat and sodium without sacrificing taste. The chart at right compares the calories, fat and sodium of a 10¾-oz. can of condensed cream of mushroom soup with the New-fashioned Cream of Mushroom Soup. Although the calories are slightly higher in the new-fashioned soup, the fat and sodium are greatly reduced.

Soup	Calories	Fat	Sodium
New-fashioned Cream of Mushroom Soup	280	6 g.	1030 mg.
10¾-oz. can Cream of Mushroom Soup	275	19 g.	2255 mg.

New-fashioned Cream Soup Mix

1¼ cups nonfat dry milk powder
 1 cup cultured buttermilk powder
 ⅓ cup cornstarch
 2 tablespoons instant chicken bouillon
   granules
 1 tablespoon dehydrated onion flakes
 1 tablespoon dried parsley flakes
 1 teaspoon garlic powder

2½ cups mix, equivalent to 5 cans
(10¾ oz. each) condensed cream soup

In large mixing bowl, combine all ingredients. Store in airtight container no longer than 6 months. Reconstitute as directed in recipes below.

TIP: For reduced-sodium diets, substitute low-sodium instant chicken bouillon granules for instant chicken bouillon granules.

Per Serving: Calories: 230 • Protein: 18 g. • Carbohydrate: 35 g.
• Fat: 2 mg. • Cholesterol: 22 mg. • Sodium: 720 mg.
Exchanges: ½ starch, ½ vegetable, 2 skim milk

Cream of Mushroom Soup

 1 teaspoon margarine or butter
 1 jar (2.5 oz.) sliced mushrooms, drained
 ½ cup New-fashioned Cream Soup Mix
   (above)
 1 cup water

About 1½ cups

In 4-cup measure, microwave margarine and mushrooms at High for 1½ to 2 minutes, or until margarine is melted, stirring once. Stir in soup mix. Blend in water. Microwave at High for 3 to 6 minutes, or until mixture thickens and bubbles, stirring after first 2 minutes and then after every minute. Use in recipes as directed.

Per Serving: Calories: 280 • Protein: 19 g. • Carbohydrate: 38 g.
• Fat: 6 g. • Cholesterol: 22 mg. • Sodium: 1030 mg.
Exchanges: ½ starch, 1½ vegetable, 2 skim milk, 1 fat

Cream of Vegetable Soup

 ½ cup New-fashioned Cream Soup Mix
   (above)
 ¼ cup dehydrated vegetable flakes
 ¼ teaspoon dried thyme or summer savory
   leaves (optional)
1¼ cups water

About 1½ cups

In 4-cup measure, combine soup mix, vegetable flakes and thyme. Blend in water. Microwave at High for 3 to 6 minutes, or until mixture thickens and bubbles, stirring after first 2 minutes and then after every minute. Let stand, covered, for 5 minutes. Use in recipes as directed.

Per Serving: Calories: 240 • Protein: 18 g. • Carbohydrate: 38 g.
• Fat: 2 g. • Cholesterol: 22 mg. • Sodium: 730 mg.
Exchanges: ½ starch, 1½ vegetable, 2 skim milk

Cream of Celery Soup

 1 teaspoon margarine or
   butter
 1 cup sliced celery

 ½ cup New-fashioned Cream
   Soup Mix (above)
 ¼ teaspoon celery seed
 1 cup water

About 1½ cups

In 4-cup measure, place margarine and celery. Cover with plastic wrap. Microwave at High for 2 to 3 minutes, or until celery is tender, stirring twice. Stir in soup mix and celery seed. Blend in water. Microwave at High for 3 to 6 minutes, or until mixture thickens and bubbles, stirring after first 2 minutes and then after every minute. Let stand, covered, for 5 minutes. Use in recipes as directed.

Per Serving: Calories: 290 • Protein: 19 g. • Carbohydrate: 40 g. • Fat: 6 g.
• Cholesterol: 22 mg. • Sodium: 870 mg.
Exchanges: ½ starch, 1½ vegetable, 2 skim milk, 1 fat

Cream of Chicken Soup

 ½ cup New-fashioned Cream
   Soup Mix (above)
1¼ cups water

About 1½ cups

In 4-cup measure, combine soup mix with water. Microwave at High for 3 to 6 minutes, or until mixture thickens and bubbles, stirring after first 2 minutes and then after every minute. Use in recipes as directed.

Per Serving: Calories: 230 • Protein: 18 g.
• Carbohydrate: 35 g. • Fat: 2 g.
• Cholesterol: 22 mg. • Sodium: 730 mg.
Exchanges: ½ starch, ½ vegetable,
2 skim milk

Hamburger & Wild Rice Casserole

1 cup uncooked wild rice
¼ cup slivered almonds
1 lb. extra-lean ground beef, crumbled
2 cups sliced fresh mushrooms (8 oz.)
1 cup sliced celery
1 tablespoon margarine or butter
1 cup New-fashioned Cream Soup Mix, page 63
1¾ cups water

4 to 6 servings

Prepare wild rice as directed on package. Drain. Set aside. In 10-inch nonstick skillet, cook almonds conventionally over medium heat just until golden brown, stirring constantly. Remove from heat. Set almonds aside. In same skillet, brown ground beef conventionally over medium heat. Drain. Set aside.

In 2-quart casserole, combine mushrooms, celery and margarine. Cover. Microwave at High for 6 to 7 minutes, or until vegetables are tender-crisp. Stir in soup mix. Blend in water. Microwave at High, uncovered, for 7 to 13 minutes, or until mixture thickens and bubbles, stirring every 2 minutes. Add rice and ground beef. Mix well. Cover. Microwave at High for 5 to 7 minutes, or until hot, stirring twice. Sprinkle with almonds.

Per Serving: Calories: 370 • Protein: 26 g. • Carbohydrate: 34 g. • Fat: 15 g.
• Cholesterol: 54 mg. • Sodium: 320 mg.
Exchanges: 1½ starch, 2½ medium-fat meat, 1 vegetable, ½ skim milk

▲ **Update Extra:** Prepare recipe as directed, except add ½ cup each green and red pepper strips to vegetable mixture before microwaving.

Chicken à la King Casserole

2 boneless whole chicken breasts (8 to 10 oz. each), skin removed, cut into ¾-inch cubes

½ cup chopped green pepper

1 jar (2 oz.) sliced pimiento, drained

1 jar (2 oz.) sliced mushrooms, drained

1 teaspoon margarine or butter

½ cup New-fashioned Cream Soup Mix, page 63

2 tablespoons all-purpose flour

1 cup water

½ cup skim milk

1 pkg. (7.5 oz.) refrigerated buttermilk biscuits, cut into quarters

Paprika

4 to 6 servings

Heat conventional oven to 350°F. In 10-inch deep-dish pie plate or 1½-quart casserole, combine chicken, green pepper, pimiento, mushrooms and margarine. Microwave at High for 4 to 8 minutes, or until meat is no longer pink, stirring 2 or 3 times. Stir in soup mix and flour. Blend in water and milk. Microwave at High for 6 to 11 minutes, or just until mixture begins to thicken, stirring every 2 minutes. Arrange biscuit quarters pointed-sides-up on top of chicken mixture. Sprinkle with paprika. Bake conventionally for 18 to 20 minutes, or until biscuits are golden brown.

Per Serving: Calories: 260 • Protein: 27 g.
• Carbohydrate: 26 g. • Fat: 5 g.
• Cholesterol: 59 mg. • Sodium: 530 mg.
Exchanges: 1 starch, 2½ lean meat,
2 vegetable

New Classics Chicken & Rice Casserole

1 recipe Cream of Mushroom
   Soup, page 63
1½ cups water
1 cup uncooked long-grain
   white rice
1 cup thinly sliced celery
⅓ cup sour cream dairy blend
2 teaspoons dried parsley
   flakes
½ teaspoon dried oregano,
   thyme or marjoram leaves
   (optional)
¼ teaspoon salt
2½ to 3-lb. broiler-fryer chicken,
   cut into quarters, skin
   removed

4 to 6 servings

Heat conventional oven to 375°F. Prepare soup as directed. Pour into 13 × 9-inch baking dish. Add remaining ingredients, except chicken. Mix well. Arrange chicken pieces on top of rice mixture. Cover with foil. Bake conventionally for 1 hour. Remove foil. Continue baking for 15 to 20 minutes, or until rice is tender and liquid is absorbed.

Per Serving: Calories: 300 • Protein: 24 g. • Carbohydrate: 34 g. • Fat: 7 g.
• Cholesterol: 60 mg. • Sodium: 350 mg.
Exchanges: 2 starch, 2 lean meat, 1 vegetable

▲ **Update Extra:** Prepare recipe as directed, except omit celery, sour cream, oregano and salt. In 2-quart casserole, prepare soup as directed. Add 1 pkg. (16 oz.) frozen broccoli, carrots, water chestnuts and red pepper and 1 tablespoon soy sauce to thickened soup mixture. Microwave at High for 4 to 5 minutes, or until vegetables are defrosted and mixture is hot, stirring twice. Continue with recipe as directed.

Light & Healthy Turkey Tetrazzini

- 1 recipe Cream of Mushroom Soup, page 63
- 8 oz. uncooked spaghetti
- ½ cup chopped celery
- 1 tablespoon water
- 1½ cups cubed fully cooked turkey or ham (¾-inch cubes)
- ½ cup shredded reduced-fat Swiss cheese (4.8 g. fat per oz.)
- ¼ cup skim milk
- 1 jar (2 oz.) sliced pimiento, drained
- ¼ teaspoon salt
- ¼ teaspoon pepper

6 servings

Heat conventional oven to 350°F. Prepare soup as directed. Set aside. Prepare spaghetti as directed on package. Rinse and drain. Set aside.

In 2-quart casserole, combine celery and water. Cover. Microwave at High for 2 to 3 minutes, or until tender-crisp, stirring once. Add spaghetti, soup and remaining ingredients. Toss to combine. Bake conventionally for 30 to 35 minutes, or until hot.

Per Serving: Calories: 280 • Protein: 22 g.
• Carbohydrate: 36 g. • Fat: 5 g.
• Cholesterol: 37 mg. • Sodium: 320 mg.
Exchanges: 2 starch, 1½ lean meat, ½ low-fat milk

▶ **Update Extra:** Prepare recipe as directed, except cut thin slice from stem end of 6 medium tomatoes (about 8 oz. each). Scoop out and discard pulp and seeds, leaving ¼-inch shells. Spoon tetrazzini mixture evenly into each tomato. Spoon remaining tetrazzini mixture into bottom of greased 11 × 7-inch baking dish. Arrange tomatoes in baking dish. Cover with foil. Bake conventionally for 40 to 50 minutes, or until hot.

Lighten-up
Tuna-Noodle Casserole

1 recipe Cream of Celery
   Soup, page 63
¼ cup skim milk
¼ cup sour cream dairy blend
¼ teaspoon salt
3 cups uncooked yolk-free
   macaroni ribbons
   (about 6 oz.)
1 cup frozen peas
1 can (8 oz.) sliced water
   chestnuts, rinsed and
   drained
1 can (6½ oz.) solid white
   tuna, water pack, drained
   and flaked
1 jar (2 oz.) sliced pimiento,
   drained

4 servings

In 2-quart casserole, prepare
soup as directed. Blend in milk,
sour cream and salt. Set aside.
Prepare macaroni as directed
on package. Rinse and drain.
Add to soup mixture. Add remaining ingredients. Mix well. Cover.
Microwave at High for 8 to 10
minutes, or until hot, stirring twice.

Per Serving: Calories: 380 • Protein: 26 g.
• Carbohydrate: 58 g. • Fat: 4 g.
• Cholesterol: 16 mg. • Sodium: 570 mg.
Exchanges: 3 starch, 1½ lean meat,
1 vegetable, ½ skim milk

◄ **Update Extra:** Prepare recipe
as directed, except substitute
1 cup thinly sliced zucchini
for peas and ½ cup seeded
chopped tomato for pimiento.

Grandma's Meatless Goulash

1 pkg. (7 oz.) uncooked elbow macaroni
1½ cups chopped green pepper
1 cup chopped onions
1 tablespoon chili powder
1 teaspoon ground cumin
½ teaspoon garlic powder
¼ teaspoon crushed red pepper flakes
1 can (16 oz.) pinto beans, rinsed and drained
1 can (14½ oz.) diced tomatoes, drained
1 can (8 oz.) tomato sauce
¼ cup plus 2 tablespoons shredded reduced-fat Cheddar cheese (5 g. fat per oz.)

6 servings

Prepare macaroni as directed on package. Rinse and drain. Set aside. In 2-quart casserole, combine green pepper, onions, chili powder, cumin, garlic powder and red pepper flakes. Cover. Microwave at High for 5 to 7 minutes, or until vegetables are tender, stirring once. Add macaroni and remaining ingredients, except cheese. Mix well. Re-cover. Microwave at High for 10 to 12 minutes, or until hot, stirring twice. Sprinkle with cheese. Microwave at High, uncovered, for 2 to 3 minutes, or until cheese is melted, rotating casserole once.

Per Serving: Calories: 250 • Protein: 12 g. • Carbohydrate: 47 g. • Fat: 3 g.
• Cholesterol: 0 • Sodium: 300 mg.
Exchanges: 2 starch, 3 vegetable, ½ fat

▲ **Update Extra:** Prepare recipe as directed, except set cooked macaroni aside. Add 1½ cups frozen corn to remaining ingredients. Cover. Microwave at High for 6 to 10 minutes, or until hot, stirring twice. To serve, place about ½ cup macaroni in each of 6 individual serving bowls. Spoon about 1 cup goulash over macaroni. Sprinkle each serving evenly with 1 tablespoon cheese. If necessary, microwave individual servings at High for 45 seconds to 1 minute, or until cheese is melted.

Trimmed-down Taco Bake

½ lb. extra-lean ground beef, crumbled
½ cup chopped green pepper
½ cup chopped onion
1 can (15 oz.) pinto beans, rinsed and drained
1 can (8 oz.) tomato sauce
½ cup salsa

2 teaspoons chili powder
½ cup sour cream dairy blend
⅓ cup shredded reduced-fat Cheddar cheese (5 g. fat per oz.)
1 cup unsalted tortilla chips, coarsely crushed

4 servings

Heat conventional oven to 350°F. In 10-inch deep-dish pie plate, combine ground beef, green pepper and onion. Microwave at High for 4 to 5 minutes, or until meat is no longer pink, stirring once to break meat apart. Drain. Add beans, tomato sauce, salsa and chili powder. Mix well. Set aside.

In small mixing bowl, combine sour cream and cheese. Spread over meat mixture to within 1 inch of edge. Sprinkle chips around outside edge. Bake conventionally for 25 to 30 minutes, or until sour cream mixture is set and casserole is hot.

Per Serving: Calories: 370 • Protein: 23 g. • Carbohydrate: 38 g. • Fat: 14 g.
• Cholesterol: 40 mg. • Sodium: 720 mg.
Exchanges: 1½ starch, 2 medium-fat meat, 3 vegetable, ½ fat

Tomato & Pesto Sauced ▲ Spinach Manicotti

8 uncooked manicotti shells
1 pkg. (0.5 oz.) pesto mix
¼ cup water
1 can (14½ oz.) diced tomatoes, drained
1 can (8 oz.) tomato sauce
1 pkg. (9 oz.) frozen chopped spinach
1 cup nonfat cottage cheese
¼ cup unseasoned dry bread crumbs
1 egg white
½ cup shredded reduced-fat mozzarella cheese (3 g. fat per oz.)

4 servings

Per Serving: Calories: 270 • Protein: 20 g.
• Carbohydrate: 43 g. • Fat: 4 g.
• Cholesterol: 7 mg. • Sodium: 820 mg.
Exchanges: 2 starch, 1 lean meat, 2½ vegetable

How to Microwave Tomato & Pesto Sauced Spinach Manicotti

Prepare manicotti as directed on package. Rinse and drain. Set aside. In 1-cup measure, combine pesto mix and water.

Combine tomatoes, tomato sauce and 1 tablespoon pesto mixture in small mixing bowl. Set aside tomato mixture and remaining pesto mixture.

Place spinach in 2-quart casserole. Cover. Microwave at High for 4 to 6 minutes, or until defrosted, stirring once to break apart. Drain, pressing to remove excess moisture.

Return spinach to 2-quart casserole. Add remaining pesto mixture, the cottage cheese, bread crumbs and egg white. Mix well. Stuff each manicotti shell with ¼ cup spinach mixture.

Arrange shells in 11 × 7-inch baking dish. Spoon tomato mixture over shells. Cover with wax paper or microwave cooking paper. Microwave at 70% (Medium High) for 12 to 15 minutes, or until manicotti is hot, rotating dish twice.

Sprinkle with mozzarella. Microwave at 70% (Medium High), uncovered, for 3 to 4 minutes, or until cheese is melted.

Enlightened Quiche

    1 pkg. (15 oz.) refrigerated
      prepared pie crusts
    1 carton (15 oz.) lite ricotta
      cheese (1 g. fat per oz.)
    1 carton (8 oz.) Egg Beaters®,
      defrosted
    1 cup skim milk
 1½ teaspoons salt-free lemon
      herb seasoning
    1 cup sliced fresh
      mushrooms (4 oz.)
  ¼ cup sliced green onions
    2 cups torn fresh spinach
      leaves

6 servings

Heat conventional oven to 375°F.
Let 1 pie crust stand at room
temperature for 15 to 20 minutes.
Reserve remaining pie crust for
future use. Unfold crust and ease
into 9-inch pie plate. Flute edge.
Set aside.

In medium mixing bowl, combine ricotta, Egg Beaters, skim
milk and seasoning. Set mixture
aside. In 1-quart casserole, combine mushrooms and onions.
Cover. Microwave at High for 2
to 4 minutes, or until mushrooms
are tender, stirring once. Add
spinach. Re-cover. Microwave
at High for 45 seconds to 1 minute, or until spinach is wilted.
Drain. Add to egg mixture. Mix
well. Pour into prepared pie shell.
Bake conventionally for 45 to
50 minutes, or until center is set.
Let stand for 10 minutes.

Per Serving: Calories: 260 • Protein: 13 g.
• Carbohydrate: 25 g. • Fat: 12 g.
• Cholesterol: 20 mg. • Sodium: 290 mg.
Exchanges: 1 starch, 1 medium-fat meat,
2 vegetable, 1½ fat

New American Classic Macaroni & Cheese

2 cups uncooked elbow macaroni
1/3 cup all-purpose flour
1 teaspoon dry mustard
1/4 teaspoon salt
1/4 teaspoon cayenne
2½ cups evaporated skim milk or skim milk
2 cups shredded reduced-fat sharp Cheddar cheese (5 g. fat per oz.)
1/4 cup unseasoned dry bread crumbs (optional)

6 to 8 servings

Heat conventional oven to 350°F. Prepare macaroni as directed on package. Rinse and drain. Set aside. In 2-quart casserole, combine flour, mustard, salt and cayenne. Blend in milk. Microwave at High for 8 to 10 minutes, or until mixture thickens and bubbles, stirring twice. Add macaroni and cheese. Mix well. Sprinkle evenly with bread crumbs. Bake conventionally for 30 to 35 minutes, or until bread crumbs are lightly toasted and casserole is hot.

Per Serving: Calories: 260 • Protein: 18 g. • Carbohydrate: 33 g. • Fat: 6 g.
• Cholesterol: 3 mg. • Sodium: 370 mg.
Exchanges: 2 starch, 1 lean meat, ½ low-fat milk

▲ **Update Extra:** Prepare recipe as directed, except add 1 pkg. (16 oz.) frozen broccoli, cauliflower and carrots to thickened milk mixture. Microwave at High for 3 to 4 minutes, or until vegetables are defrosted, stirring once. Continue with recipe as directed.

Stroganoff with a Light Difference ▶

2 cups uncooked yolk-free
   macaroni ribbons
   (about 4 oz.)
   Nonstick vegetable cooking
   spray

¾-lb. boneless beef sirloin
   steak, about ¾ inch thick,
   cut into thin strips
2 cloves garlic, minced
8 oz. fresh mushrooms, sliced
   (2 cups)
½ cup chopped onion
¼ cup all-purpose flour

¼ teaspoon salt
1 cup ready-to-serve beef
   broth
2 tablespoons dry sherry
2 tablespoons catsup
¼ cup snipped fresh parsley
⅓ cup sour cream dairy blend

4 servings

How to Make Stroganoff with a Light Difference

Prepare macaroni as directed on package. Rinse and drain. Set aside. Spray 10-inch skillet with nonstick vegetable cooking spray. Heat conventionally over medium-high heat.

Add beef strips and garlic. Sauté for 4 to 5 minutes, or until meat is lightly browned. Set aside.

Combine mushrooms and onion in 2-quart casserole. Cover. Microwave at High for 6 to 9 minutes, or until vegetables are tender, stirring once or twice. Drain. Set aside.

Combine flour and salt in 2-cup measure. Blend in broth, sherry and catsup. Add to vegetables. Microwave at High, uncovered, for 4 to 8 minutes, or until mixture thickens and bubbles, stirring 2 or 3 times.

Add macaroni, beef strips and parsley. Mix well. Microwave at High for 2 to 4 minutes, or until hot, stirring once. Add sour cream. Toss to coat. Garnish with additional parsley, if desired.

Per Serving: Calories: 280 • Protein: 24 g. • Carbohydrate: 31 g. • Fat: 6 g. • Cholesterol: 53 mg. • Sodium: 500 mg. Exchanges: 1½ starch, 2½ lean meat, 1½ vegetable

Update Extra: Prepare recipe as directed, except substitute 3-quart casserole for 2-quart casserole. Add 1 pkg. (16 oz.) frozen broccoli, cauliflower and carrots to mushrooms and onion mixture. Microwave at High for 9 to 14 minutes, or until vegetables are tender, stirring once. Drain. Continue with recipe as directed.

74

Lean Vegetable Lasagna ▲

- 9 uncooked lasagna noodles
- 1 recipe Cream of Vegetable Soup, page 63
- 3 cups frozen broccoli cuts
- 2 cups shredded carrots
- 2 cups green and red pepper strips (2 × ¼-inch strips)
- ½ cup chopped onion
- 1 clove garlic, minced
- 1 can (14½ oz.) diced tomatoes, drained
- 1 carton (16 oz.) lite ricotta cheese (1 g. fat per oz.)
- ½ cup snipped fresh parsley
- 1 egg white
- 1½ cups shredded reduced-fat mozzarella cheese (3 g. fat per oz.)

8 servings

Per Serving: Calories: 260 • Protein: 20 g.
• Carbohydrate: 35 g. • Fat: 5 g.
• Cholesterol: 17 mg. • Sodium: 280 mg.
Exchanges: 1 starch, 1½ lean meat, 4 vegetable

How to Make Lean Vegetable Lasagna

Heat conventional oven to 350°F. Prepare lasagna noodles as directed on package. Rinse. Let stand in warm water. Prepare soup as directed. Set aside.

Combine broccoli, carrots, pepper strips, onion and garlic in 3-quart casserole. Cover. Microwave at High for 8 to 10 minutes, or until vegetables are tender, stirring once. Drain.

Lean Meat Lasagna

9 uncooked lasagna noodles
1 lb. extra-lean ground beef, crumbled
½ cup chopped onion
1 clove garlic, minced
1 can (16 oz.) whole tomatoes, undrained and cut up
1 can (8 oz.) tomato sauce
1 can (6 oz.) tomato paste
1 teaspoon sugar
½ teaspoon dried basil leaves
¼ teaspoon fennel seed, crushed
1 carton (16 oz.) lite ricotta cheese (1 g. fat per oz.)
½ cup snipped fresh parsley
1 egg white
1½ cups shredded reduced-fat mozzarella cheese, divided (3 g. fat per oz.)

8 servings

Heat conventional oven to 350°F. Prepare lasagna noodles as directed on package. Rinse. Let stand in warm water. In 2-quart casserole, combine ground beef, onion and garlic. Microwave at High for 5 to 7 minutes, or until meat is no longer pink, stirring twice to break meat apart. Drain. Add tomatoes, tomato sauce, tomato paste, sugar, basil and fennel. Mix well. Set aside.

In small mixing bowl, combine ricotta, parsley and egg white. Mix well. Place lasagna noodles on paper towels to drain. In 13 × 9-inch baking dish, layer 3 noodles, 1⅓ cups meat mixture, half of ricotta mixture and ½ cup mozzarella. Top with 3 noodles, 1⅓ cups meat mixture, remaining ricotta mixture and ½ cup mozzarella. Top with remaining noodles and meat mixture. Cover with foil. Bake conventionally for 40 to 45 minutes, or until lasagna is hot. Remove foil. Sprinkle with remaining ½ cup mozzarella. Bake for 5 to 10 minutes, or until cheese is melted.

Per Serving: Calories: 340 • Protein: 28 g. • Carbohydrate: 31 g. • Fat: 11 g.
• Cholesterol: 50 mg. • Sodium: 620 mg.
Exchanges: 1 starch, 2½ medium-fat meat, 3 fat

Add tomatoes. Mix well. Set aside. In small mixing bowl, combine ricotta, parsley and egg white. Set aside. Place lasagna noodles on paper towels to drain.

Layer 3 noodles, 2 cups vegetable mixture, half of ricotta mixture and ½ cup mozzarella in 13 × 9-inch baking dish. Top with 3 noodles, 2 cups vegetable mixture, remaining ricotta mixture and ½ cup mozzarella.

Top with remaining noodles, the soup and remaining vegetable mixture. Cover with foil. Bake conventionally for 35 to 40 minutes, or until lasagna is hot. Remove foil. Sprinkle with remaining ½ cup mozzarella. Bake for 5 to 10 minutes, or until cheese is melted.

1. Microwave vegetables.

2. Pan-fry.

3. Add sauce.

Speedy Casseroles: Techniques

This section takes two different approaches to timesaving casseroles. For days when you arrive home with only minutes to spare before dinner, rely on your microwave oven to help you prepare and heat a meal in minutes. When you have more time at home but no time to cook, start your casserole in the microwave, then pop it into a conventional oven and walk away.

Convenience products, used as basic ingredients, speed preparation. Combine them with fresh foods from the refrigerator and items from the pantry to create "from scratch" casseroles.

Microwave cooking delivers dinner in a flash. Superspeedy all-microwave casseroles cook in 15 minutes or less.

Combo cooking starts with the microwave for speedy preparation. Attention-free conventional baking takes 20 to 50 minutes, leaving you time to attend to other activities.

Salmon Succotash Soufflé

⅓ cup chopped green
    pepper
⅓ cup chopped red pepper
1 cup frozen corn
2 tablespoons margarine or
    butter
¼ cup all-purpose flour
½ teaspoon dried dill weed
¼ teaspoon salt
⅛ teaspoon pepper
1½ cups milk
4 egg yolks, beaten
1 can (6½ oz.) skinless,
    boneless salmon, drained
5 egg whites

4 servings

Heat conventional oven to 350°F. Grease 2-quart soufflé dish. Set aside. In medium mixing bowl, combine chopped peppers, corn and margarine. Cover with plastic wrap. Microwave at High for 4 to 6 minutes, or until vegetables are tender, stirring once. Stir in flour, dill weed, salt and pepper. Blend in milk.

Microwave at High, uncovered, for 6 to 8½ minutes, or until mixture thickens and bubbles, stirring every 2 minutes. Stir small amount of hot mixture gradually into egg yolks. Blend yolks back into hot mixture. Add salmon. Mix well. Set aside.

In large mixing bowl, beat egg whites at high speed of electric mixer until stiff but not dry. Fold into salmon mixture. Pour mixture into prepared dish. Bake conventionally for 45 to 50 minutes, or until soufflé is golden brown and knife inserted in center comes out clean.

Per Serving: Calories: 310 • Protein: 20 g. • Carbohydrate: 21 g. • Fat: 16 g.
• Cholesterol: 241 mg. • Sodium: 530 mg.
Exchanges: 1 starch, 2 medium-fat meat, ½ low-fat milk, ½ fat

Corn Bread Creole

½ cup chopped celery
½ cup chopped green pepper
1 tablespoon margarine or butter
1 jar (15½ oz.) spaghetti sauce
1 pkg. (10 oz.) frozen cooked shrimp, defrosted
2 tablespoons snipped fresh parsley
¼ teaspoon cayenne
¼ teaspoon dried oregano leaves
¼ teaspoon dried thyme leaves
1 pkg. (8½ oz.) corn muffin mix
⅓ cup milk
1 egg, beaten
5 green, red or yellow pepper rings

6 servings

Heat conventional oven to 350°F. In 8-inch square baking dish, combine celery, chopped pepper and margarine. Cover with plastic wrap. Microwave at High for 3 to 4 minutes, or until vegetables are tender, stirring once. Add spaghetti sauce, shrimp, parsley, cayenne, oregano and thyme. Mix well. Set aside.

In medium mixing bowl, combine corn muffin mix, milk and egg. Spoon evenly over shrimp mixture. Arrange pepper rings over corn bread. Bake conventionally for 30 to 35 minutes, or until golden brown.

Per Serving: Calories: 330 • Protein: 15 g. • Carbohydrate: 42 g. • Fat: 11 g.
• Cholesterol: 129 mg. • Sodium: 750 mg.
Exchanges: 2 starch, 1 lean meat, 2½ vegetable, 1½ fat

1. Cook pasta.

2. Add tomatoes.

3. Add cheese and chilies.

◀ Mexican Bow-tie Macaroni & Cheese

8 oz. uncooked bow-tie pasta (3 cups)
1 can (14½ oz.) diced tomatoes, drained
8 oz. pasteurized process American cheese loaf, cut into ½-inch cubes
1 can (4 oz.) chopped green chilies, drained

4 servings

Prepare pasta as directed on package. Rinse and drain. In 2-quart casserole, combine pasta, tomatoes, cheese and chilies. Microwave at High for 6 to 13 minutes, or until cheese is melted and mixture is hot, stirring 2 or 3 times.

Per Serving: Calories: 440 • Protein: 21 g.
• Carbohydrate: 47 g. • Fat: 19 g.
• Cholesterol: 54 mg. • Sodium: 820 mg.
Exchanges: 2 starch, 2 high-fat meat, 3 vegetable

Turkey-Noodle Paprikash ▲

3 cups uncooked mini lasagna noodles
1 lb. ground turkey, crumbled
½ cup chopped onion
1 cup frozen peas
1 can (10¾ oz.) condensed cream of mushroom soup

2 tablespoons white wine
1 tablespoon paprika
¼ teaspoon salt
⅛ teaspoon pepper
½ cup sour cream

6 servings

Prepare noodles as directed on package. Rinse and drain. Set aside. In 2-quart casserole, combine turkey and onion. Microwave at High for 4 to 7 minutes, or until meat is no longer pink, stirring twice to break apart. Drain. Add noodles and peas. Set aside.

In small mixing bowl, combine remaining ingredients, except sour cream. Add to turkey mixture. Mix well. Cover. Microwave at High for 6 to 8 minutes, or until mixture is hot, stirring twice. Add sour cream. Mix well.

Per Serving: Calories: 340 • Protein: 22 g. • Carbohydrate: 31 g. • Fat: 14 g.
• Cholesterol: 60 mg. • Sodium: 590 mg.
Exchanges: 2 starch, 2½ lean meat, 1 fat

Quick Sole Florentine for Two ▲

Nonstick vegetable cooking
  spray
1 pkg. (12 oz.) frozen
  spinach soufflé
2 tablespoons margarine or
  butter
1 tablespoon lemon juice
½ cup cornflake crumbs

¼ teaspoon salt
¼ teaspoon pepper
4 sole fillets (2 oz. each)
¼ cup shredded Cheddar
  cheese
½ cup quartered cherry
  tomatoes
¼ cup sliced green onions

2 servings

Heat conventional oven to 400°F. Spray 8-inch square baking dish
with nonstick vegetable cooking spray. Set aside. Place spinach
soufflé in 1-quart casserole. Cover. Microwave at 50% (Medium) for
4 to 6 minutes, or until defrosted, stirring once. Spread evenly into
prepared baking dish. Set aside.

In 9-inch pie plate, microwave margarine at High for 45 seconds
to 1 minute, or until melted. Add juice. Mix well. On piece of wax paper
or microwave cooking paper, combine crumbs, salt and pepper. Dip
each fillet in margarine mixture. Dredge in cornflake mixture, pressing lightly to coat. Arrange fillets over spinach soufflé. Bake conventionally for 15 to 17 minutes, or until fish flakes easily with fork. Sprinkle
evenly with cheese. Bake for 2 to 3 minutes, or until cheese is melted.
In small mixing bowl, combine tomatoes and onions. Spoon evenly
over each serving.

Per Serving: Calories: 570 • Protein: 36 g. • Carbohydrate: 33 g. • Fat: 31 g.
• Cholesterol: N/A • Sodium: 1560 mg.
Exchanges: 1 starch, 3½ medium-fat meat, 3½ vegetable, 3 fat

Cheesy Turkey & Chili Roll-ups

4 flour tortillas (8-inch)
4 slices Cheddar cheese
  (1 oz. each)
8 slices fully cooked turkey or
  chicken breast (1 oz. each)
1 can (4 oz.) whole green
  chilies, drained
1 can (10 oz.) enchilada sauce

4 servings

In center of each tortilla, place
1 cheese slice, 2 turkey slices
and 1 chili. Roll up tortillas to
enclose filling. Arrange in 8-inch
square baking dish. Pour enchilida
sauce over tortillas. Microwave
at 70% (Medium High) for 10 to
12 minutes, or until cheese is
melted and tortillas are hot, rotating dish 2 or 3 times. Serve
sprinkled with chopped tomato
and onion and dollops of sour
cream, if desired.

Per Serving: Calories: 390 • Protein: 27 g.
• Carbohydrate: 32 g. • Fat: 17 g.
• Cholesterol: 73 mg. • Sodium: 710 mg.
Exchanges: 1½ starch, 2½ medium-fat
meat, 2 vegetable, 1 fat

Crescent Turkey ▶
& Vegetable Bake

- 1 pkg. (1.8 oz.) white sauce mix
- ½ teaspoon poultry seasoning
- 2¼ cups milk
- 1 pkg. (16 oz.) frozen broccoli, cauliflower and carrots
- 1½ cups shredded fully cooked turkey
- 1 pkg. (8 oz.) refrigerated crescent roll dough
  Paprika

4 to 6 servings

Heat conventional oven to 350°F. In 11 × 7-inch baking dish or 10-inch square casserole, combine white sauce mix and poultry seasoning. Blend in milk. Microwave at High for 11 to 13 minutes, or until mixture thickens and bubbles, stirring 3 times. Add vegetables and turkey. Cover with plastic wrap. Microwave at High for 9 to 12 minutes, or until hot, stirring twice.

Roll up crescent rolls as directed on package. Arrange on top of turkey mixture. Sprinkle with paprika. Bake conventionally for 17 to 20 minutes, or until rolls are deep golden brown and mixture is hot.

Per Serving: Calories: 300 • Protein: 18 g.
• Carbohydrate: 27 g. • Fat: 14 g.
• Cholesterol: 34 mg. • Sodium: 630 mg.
Exchanges: 1 starch, 1 lean meat,
1 vegetable, ½ low-fat milk, 1½ fat

Stuffed Turkey Breast Casserole

- 1 pkg. (6 oz.) chicken-flavored stuffing mix
- 6 slices fresh turkey breast (2.5 to 3 oz. each)
- ½ cup prepared turkey gravy

6 servings

Prepare stuffing mix as directed on package. Spoon ½ cup stuffing onto one end of each turkey slice. Fold remaining end of turkey slice over stuffing to enclose. Arrange stuffed slices in 8-inch square baking dish with folded sides toward outside edges of dish. Pour gravy evenly over turkey and stuffing. Cover with plastic wrap. Microwave at 70% (Medium High) for 6 to 8 minutes, or until meat is no longer pink, rotating dish once or twice.

Per Serving: Calories: 280 • Protein: 26 g. • Carbohydrate: 21 g. • Fat: 10 g.
• Cholesterol: 80 mg. • Sodium: 710 mg.
Exchanges: 1½ starch, 3 lean meat

Skillet Pizza Potatoes ▲

2 lbs. red potatoes, peeled and sliced
   (¼-inch slices)
½ cup chopped green pepper
½ cup chopped onion
¼ cup water
2 tablespoons vegetable oil
½ cup pepperoni slices
⅓ cup sliced pimiento-stuffed green olives
½ teaspoon Italian seasoning
¼ teaspoon salt
1 jar (15½ oz.) spaghetti sauce
1 cup shredded mozzarella cheese

4 to 6 servings

In 2-quart casserole, combine potatoes, green pepper, onion and water. Cover. Microwave at High for 10 to 12 minutes, or just until potatoes are tender, stirring 2 or 3 times. Drain. In 12-inch non-stick skillet, heat oil conventionally over medium-high heat. Add potato mixture, pepperoni, olives, Italian seasoning and salt. Cook over medium-high heat for 8 to 10 minutes, or until potatoes are browned and tender, stirring frequently. Stir in spaghetti sauce. Reduce heat to low. Sprinkle evenly with cheese. Cook for 10 to 12 minutes, or until cheese is melted and mixture is hot.

Per Serving: Calories: 370 • Protein: 13 g. • Carbohydrate: 42 g.
• Fat: 18 g. • Cholesterol: 20 mg. • Sodium: 1000 mg.
Exchanges: 1½ starch, ½ medium-fat meat, 4 vegetable, 3 fat

Instant Curried Tuna ▶

½ cup sliced green onions
2 tablespoons margarine or butter
2¼ cups uncooked instant rice
2 cans (6¼ oz. each) solid white tuna, water pack, drained and flaked
1 can (10¾ oz.) condensed cream of celery or mushroom soup
1 jar (2 oz.) sliced pimiento, drained
2 teaspoons curry powder
⅛ teaspoon cayenne
⅛ teaspoon garlic powder
1 cup milk
1 hard-cooked egg, sliced (optional)
   Toasted almond slices (optional)
   Raisins (optional)

6 servings

In 2-quart casserole, combine onions and margarine. Cover. Microwave at High for 2 to 3 minutes, or until tender, stirring once. Add rice. Add remaining ingredients, except egg, almonds and raisins. Mix well. Re-cover. Microwave at High for 8 to 10 minutes, or until liquid is absorbed and rice is tender, stirring twice. Serve topped with egg, almonds and raisins.

Per Serving: Calories: 300 • Protein: 21 g. • Carbohydrate: 37 g.
• Fat: 7 g. • Cholesterol: 19 mg. • Sodium: 650 mg.
Exchanges: 2 starch, 2 lean meat, 1 vegetable

1. Microwave onions.

2. Add rice.

3. Add remaining ingredients.

◄ Chicken-n-Rice with Peppers & Pine Nuts

- ⅓ cup pine nuts
- ½ cup chopped green pepper
- ½ cup chopped red pepper
- ⅓ cup chopped onion
- 1 tablespoon margarine or butter
- 2 cups uncooked instant rice
- 1 can (10¾ oz.) condensed cream of broccoli soup
- 2 cans (5 oz. each) chunk breast of chicken, water pack, drained
- 1 cup milk
- ¼ cup grated Parmesan cheese

6 servings

In 8-inch skillet, cook pine nuts conventionally over medium-high heat about 2 minutes, or until lightly browned, stirring frequently. Set aside. In 2-quart casserole, combine chopped peppers, onion and margarine. Cover. Microwave at High for 4 to 5 minutes, or until vegetables are tender, stirring once. Add pine nuts and remaining ingredients. Mix well. Cover. Microwave at High for 8 to 12 minutes, or until rice is tender and mixture is hot, stirring twice.

Per Serving: Calories: 330 • Protein: 18 g.
• Carbohydrate: 36 g. • Fat: 13 g.
• Cholesterol: 35 mg. • Sodium: 660 mg.
Exchanges: 1½ starch, 1 medium-fat meat, 2½ vegetable, 1½ fat

Macaroni & Cheese Primavera

- 1 pkg. (14 oz.) deluxe macaroni and cheese dinner
- 2 cups fresh broccoli flowerets
- 1 cup sliced zucchini or yellow summer squash
- ½ cup red pepper strips (1 × ¼-inch strips)
- ¼ cup water

4 to 6 servings

Prepare macaroni and cheese as directed on package. Set aside. In 2-quart casserole, combine broccoli, zucchini, red pepper and water. Cover. Microwave at High for 6 to 8 minutes, or until vegetables are tender-crisp, stirring twice. Drain. Add vegetables to macaroni and cheese. Mix well.

Per Serving: Calories: 130 • Protein: 6 g. • Carbohydrate: 19 g. • Fat: 4 g.
• Cholesterol: 9 mg. • Sodium: 270 mg.
Exchanges: ½ starch, ½ high-fat meat, 2 vegetable

Chicken Mozzarella ▲

1 pkg. (7 oz.) uncooked spaghetti, broken
    into 2-inch lengths
1 jar (15½ oz.) spaghetti sauce
4 frozen fully cooked breaded chicken patties
1 tablespoon margarine or butter
1 tablespoon all-purpose flour
⅛ teaspoon salt
⅛ teaspoon cayenne
½ cup half-and-half
1 cup shredded mozzarella cheese

4 servings

Prepare spaghetti as directed on package. Rinse
and drain. In 11 × 7-inch or 8-inch square baking dish, combine spaghetti and spaghetti sauce.
Spread evenly in baking dish. Arrange chicken
patties over spaghetti. Cover with plastic wrap.
Microwave at High for 6 to 10 minutes, or until
patties are hot, rotating dish once. Set aside. In
2-cup measure, microwave margarine at High
for 45 seconds to 1 minute, or until melted. Stir
in flour, salt and cayenne. Blend in half-and-half.
Microwave at High for 3 to 4 minutes, or until mixture thickens and bubbles, stirring twice. Add
cheese. Stir until cheese is melted. Pour sauce
evenly over chicken patties. Place under conventional broiler, 3 to 4 inches from heat. Broil
for 2 to 3 minutes, or until sauce begins to brown
and bubble.

Per Serving: Calories: 640 • Protein: 30 g. • Carbohydrate: 61 g.
• Fat: 30 g. • Cholesterol: 69 mg. • Sodium: 1020 mg.
Exchanges: 2½ starch, 2 lean meat, 4½ vegetable, 5 fat

Chicken Hash

3 cups frozen loose-pack cubed hash
    browns with chopped onions and peppers
2 tablespoons margarine or butter
2 tablespoons all-purpose flour
2 cups cubed fully cooked chicken (1-inch
    cubes)
½ cup half-and-half or whipping cream
2 tablespoons to ¼ cup white wine
½ teaspoon salt
¼ teaspoon dried sage leaves
¼ teaspoon dried thyme leaves
¼ teaspoon cayenne
2 tablespoons unseasoned dry bread crumbs
2 tablespoons grated Parmesan cheese

4 servings

Heat conventional oven to 400°F. In 2-quart
casserole, combine hash browns and margarine.
Cover. Microwave at High for 6 to 8 minutes, or
until potatoes are hot, stirring once. Add flour.
Toss to coat. Add remaining ingredients, except
bread crumbs and cheese. Mix well. In small
mixing bowl, combine bread crumbs and cheese.
Sprinkle evenly over potato mixture. Bake conventionally for 25 to 30 minutes, or until top is
golden brown and mixture is hot.

Per Serving: Calories: 380 • Protein: 26 g. • Carbohydrate: 33 g.
• Fat: 16 g. • Cholesterol: 76 mg. • Sodium: 520 mg.
Exchanges: 2 starch, 2½ lean meat, ½ vegetable, 1½ fat

Scalloped Hash Browns & Ham Casserole

1 pkg. (32 oz.) frozen loose-pack cubed hash browns
1 cup cubed fully cooked ham (½-inch cubes)
1 pkg. (1.8 oz.) white sauce mix
2¼ cups milk
1 cup shredded Cheddar cheese
½ cup sour cream with chives
¼ cup margarine or butter
2 cups cornflakes, coarsely crushed

8 servings

Heat conventional oven to 350°F. In 10-inch square casserole or 2½-quart oval casserole, combine hash browns and ham. Set aside. Place white sauce mix in 4-cup measure. Blend in milk. Microwave at High for 7 to 12 minutes, or until mixture thickens and bubbles, stirring with whisk every 2 minutes. Add cheese and sour cream. Stir until cheese is melted and mixture is smooth. Pour evenly over potato and ham mixture. Set aside. In small mixing bowl, microwave margarine at High for 1¼ to 1½ minutes, or until melted. Add cornflake crumbs. Toss to coat. Sprinkle around edges of casserole. Bake conventionally for 40 to 50 minutes, or until mixture is hot and bubbly around edges.

Per Serving: Calories: 410 • Protein: 14 g. • Carbohydrate: 45 g. • Fat: 19 g.
• Cholesterol: 36 mg. • Sodium: 810 mg.
Exchanges: 2½ starch, 1 medium-fat meat, ½ low-fat milk, 2 fat

◀ Ham & Cheese Italiano

½ cup chopped zucchini
½ cup seeded chopped tomato
½ cup chopped onion
1 teaspoon Italian seasoning
¼ teaspoon garlic powder
¼ teaspoon fennel seed, crushed
¼ teaspoon salt
⅛ teaspoon pepper
1 teaspoon olive oil
1½ cups milk
1 egg
2 cups buttermilk baking mix
1 pkg. (2.5 oz.) thinly sliced fully cooked lean ham
4 slices (1 oz. each) Cheddar cheese

6 servings

Heat conventional oven to 350°F. Grease 8-inch square baking dish. Set aside. In medium mixing bowl, combine vegetables, seasonings and oil. Cover with plastic wrap. Microwave at High for 2 to 3 minutes, or until vegetables are tender-crisp, stirring once. Add milk, egg and baking mix. Beat with whisk until mixture is well blended.

Pour half of egg mixture into prepared baking dish. Layer ham evenly over egg mixture. Top evenly with cheese slices. Pour remaining egg mixture over cheese. Bake conventionally for 45 to 50 minutes, or until mixture is set and top is golden brown. Let stand for 10 minutes before cutting.

Per Serving: Calories: 320 • Protein: 14 g.
• Carbohydrate: 29 g. • Fat: 17 g.
• Cholesterol: 66 mg. • Sodium: 770 mg.
Exchanges: 1 starch, 1 high-fat meat, 1½ vegetable, ½ low-fat milk, 1 fat

Speedy Spanish Paella

Nonstick vegetable
  cooking spray
2½ lbs. chicken wings
  ½ teaspoon garlic salt
  ½ teaspoon paprika
  1 pkg. (6.8 oz.) rice and
    vermicelli mix with
    Spanish seasoning
  2 tablespoons margarine or
    butter
2½ cups hot water
  1 can (14½ oz.) diced
    tomatoes, undrained
  1 cup frozen mixed vegetables

4 servings

Heat conventional oven to 425°F. Spray 15½ × 10½-inch baking sheet with nonstick vegetable cooking spray. Set aside. Separate each chicken wing into 3 pieces, cutting at joints. Discard wing tips. In large food-storage bag, combine garlic salt and paprika. Add chicken wings. Shake to coat. Arrange in single layer on prepared baking sheet. Bake conventionally for 30 to 40 minutes, or until golden brown, re-arranging once.

In 10-inch square casserole or 3-quart oval baking dish, combine rice and vermicelli mix, seasoning and margarine. Microwave at High for 3 to 4 minutes, or until vermicelli is lightly browned, stirring twice. Add water, tomatoes and vegetables. Cover. Microwave at High for 25 to 30 minutes, or until most of liquid is absorbed. Let stand, covered, for 5 minutes. Fluff with fork. Arrange chicken wings over rice mixture.

Per Serving: Calories: 550 • Protein: 32 g. • Carbohydrate: 48 g. • Fat: 26 g.
• Cholesterol: 76 mg. • Sodium: 2230 mg.
Exchanges: 2½ starch, 3 lean meat, 2 vegetable, 3½ fat

Sloppy Joe Bake

- 4 corn muffins
- 1 lb. lean ground beef, crumbled
- 1 cup water
- 1 can (6 oz.) tomato paste
- 1 pkg. (1.5 oz.) Sloppy Joe seasoning mix
- ½ cup shredded Cheddar cheese

4 servings

Cut each muffin crosswise into thirds. Set tops aside. Arrange remaining pieces evenly in bottom of 8-inch square baking dish. Set aside. In 2-quart casserole, microwave ground beef at High for 4 to 6 minutes, or until no longer pink, stirring twice to break apart. Drain. Add water, tomato paste and seasoning mix. Mix well. Microwave at High for 4 to 6 minutes, or until hot, stirring once. Spoon over muffin pieces. Arrange muffin tops over ground beef mixture. Sprinkle evenly with cheese. Microwave at High for 2 to 4 minutes, or until cheese is melted, rotating dish once.

Per Serving: Calories: 460 • Protein: 27 g.
• Carbohydrate: 36 g. • Fat: 23 g.
• Cholesterol: 103 mg. • Sodium: 1150 mg.
Exchanges: 2 starch, 2½ medium-fat meat, 1 vegetable, 2 fat

Chili Popover Pie ▲

- 1 lb. lean ground beef, crumbled
- 1 can (16 oz.) whole tomatoes, undrained and cut up
- 1 can (15½ oz.) kidney beans, rinsed and drained
- 1 pkg. (1.25 oz.) chili seasoning mix
- 3 eggs
- 1 cup all-purpose flour
- 1 cup milk
- 1 tablespoon margarine or butter

6 to 8 servings

Heat conventional oven to 400°F. In 2-quart casserole, microwave ground beef at High for 4 to 7 minutes, or until no longer pink, stirring twice to break apart. Drain. Add tomatoes, beans and seasoning mix. Mix well. Microwave at High for 5 to 6 minutes, or until chili is hot and slightly thickened, stirring twice. Set aside. In medium mixing bowl, combine eggs, flour and milk. Beat with whisk until mixture is smooth. Set batter aside. Place margarine in 13 × 9-inch baking dish or 3-quart oval casserole. Place in conventional oven for 3 to 5 minutes, or until melted. Tilt dish to coat bottom evenly with margarine. Pour in batter. Spoon chili mixture into dish to within 2 inches of edges. Bake conventionally for 20 to 30 minutes, or until batter is puffed and golden brown. Serve immediately.

Per Serving: Calories: 290 • Protein: 19 g. • Carbohydrate: 26 g. • Fat: 12 g.
• Cholesterol: 117 mg. • Sodium: 320 mg.
Exchanges: 1½ starch, 2 medium-fat meat, 1 vegetable

Quick & Easy Savory Meat Pie

1 pkg. (15 oz.) refrigerated prepared pie crusts
2 pkgs. (14 oz. each) frozen beef stew
3 tablespoons all-purpose flour
½ teaspoon dried marjoram leaves
½ teaspoon dried thyme leaves
¼ cup red wine
1 egg yolk
2 teaspoons water

6 servings

Heat conventional oven to 425°F. Let crusts stand at room temperature for 15 to 20 minutes. Unfold 1 crust; ease into 9-inch pie plate. Set aside. In 2-quart casserole, microwave beef stew at High for 12 to 15 minutes, or until defrosted, stirring twice to break apart. In 1-cup measure, combine flour, marjoram and thyme. Blend in wine. Add to beef stew. Mix well. Spoon beef stew mixture into pie crust. Place remaining crust over beef stew mixture and flute edge. Cut several vents in top crust. In small bowl, combine egg yolk and water. Brush top crust evenly with egg mixture. Sprinkle evenly with sesame seed or poppy seed, if desired. Bake conventionally for 25 to 30 minutes, or until crust is deep golden brown.

Per Serving: Calories: 450 • Protein: 12 g. • Carbohydrate: 43 g. • Fat: 24 g.
• Cholesterol: 70 mg. • Sodium: 1140 mg.
Exchanges: 2 starch, ½ medium-fat meat, 2½ vegetable, 4 fat

1. Assemble and refrigerate overnight.

2. Heat and serve.

Make-ahead Casseroles: Techniques

A casserole that can be assembled in advance and baked just before serving takes the fuss out of last-minute meal preparations. The recipes in this section can be prepared the night before and served at a company brunch or family dinner the next day. In fact, standing time in the refrigerator is an essential part of the preparation.

Read the recipes carefully. Some include shortcuts that may surprise you. For example, although one casserole calls for cooked macaroni, in some others pasta goes into the dish uncooked.

Uncooked pasta makes assembly fast. It is even simple to stuff manicotti. Recipes contain more liquid than usual to rehydrate pasta. These casseroles *must* be refrigerated for at least 12 hours to give pasta time to soften.

Frozen vegetables and shrimp combine quickly with other ingredients and defrost while the casserole stands in the refrigerator.

Uncooked meats and fresh vegetables should be fully cooked before the casserole is assembled.

Bake-It-Later Lasagna

- ¾ lb. bulk Italian sausage
- 2 cups sliced fresh mushrooms (8 oz.)
- 1 cup chopped zucchini
- 1 can (28 oz.) whole tomatoes, undrained and cut up
- 1 can (15 oz.) tomato purée
- 1 can (6 oz.) tomato paste
- 2 teaspoons dried oregano leaves
- ½ teaspoon salt
- ½ teaspoon sugar
- 1 carton (15 oz.) ricotta cheese
- ½ cup grated fresh Parmesan cheese
- 1 tablespoon dried parsley flakes
- ½ teaspoon garlic powder
- 9 uncooked lasagna noodles
- 1 pkg. (8 oz.) sliced mozzarella cheese

8 servings

Per Serving: Calories: 400 • Protein: 27 g.
• Carbohydrate: 37 g. • Fat: 17 g.
• Cholesterol: 52 mg. • Sodium: 1190 mg.
Exchanges: 1½ starch, 2½ medium-fat meat, 3 vegetable, ½ fat

How to Make Bake-It-Later Lasagna

Combine sausage, mushrooms and zucchini in 2-quart casserole. Microwave at High for 6 to 10 minutes, or until meat is no longer pink, stirring twice to break meat apart. Drain.

Add tomatoes, tomato purée, tomato paste, oregano, salt and sugar. Mix well. Set aside. In small mixing bowl, combine ricotta, Parmesan cheese, parsley and garlic.

Place 3 lasagna noodles in single layer in bottom of 11 × 7-inch baking dish. Top with half of meat sauce.

Toasted Ham
& Cheesy Vegetable Casserole

1 pkg. (16 oz.) frozen broccoli cuts
1 pkg. (9 oz.) frozen mixed vegetables
¾ lb. fully cooked ham, cut into ½-inch cubes
¼ cup margarine or butter, divided
½ cup chopped onion
⅓ cup all-purpose flour
1 teaspoon dry mustard
½ teaspoon salt
¼ teaspoon garlic powder
3 cups milk
8 oz. pasteurized process cheese loaf, cut
   into 1-inch cubes
4 cups sourdough bread cubes (1-inch cubes)

8 servings

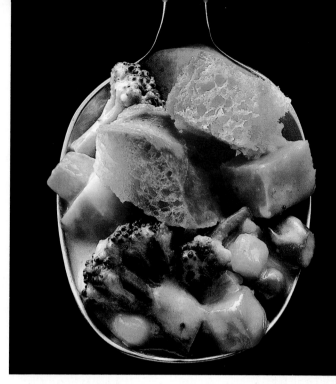

In 11 × 7-inch baking dish, layer broccoli, vegetables and ham. Set aside. In 2-quart casserole, place 2 tablespoons margarine and the onion. Microwave at High for 2 to 4 minutes, or until onion is tender, stirring once. Stir in flour, mustard, salt and garlic powder. Blend in milk.

Microwave at High for 10 to 15 minutes, or until mixture thickens and bubbles, stirring every 2 minutes. Add cheese. Stir until melted. Spoon cheese sauce mixture evenly over vegetable mixture. Cover with plastic wrap and refrigerate up to 12 hours or overnight. In medium mixing bowl, melt

remaining 2 tablespoons margarine at High for 45 seconds to 1 minute. Add bread cubes. Toss to coat. Cover and refrigerate 12 hours or overnight.

Heat conventional oven to 350°F. Remove plastic wrap from casserole. Sprinkle casserole evenly with bread cubes. Bake, uncovered, for 50 minutes to 1 hour, or until casserole is hot and golden brown.

Per Serving: Calories: 390 • Protein: 24 g. • Carbohydrate: 30 g. • Fat: 19 g. • Cholesterol: 56 mg. • Sodium: 1320 mg.
Exchanges: 1½ starch, 2½ medium-fat meat, 1½ vegetable, 1 fat

Arrange 3 more noodles over sauce. Top with 2 mozzarella cheese slices and the ricotta mixture. Top with remaining noodles and meat sauce.

Arrange remaining cheese slices over meat sauce. Cover with plastic wrap. Refrigerate 12 hours or overnight.

Heat conventional oven to 350°F. Remove plastic wrap and cover with foil. Bake for 30 minutes. Remove foil. Bake for 45 minutes to 1 hour, or until hot and bubbly. Let stand for 15 minutes before cutting.

Ham & Cheese Sandwich Bake

3 tablespoons margarine or butter
12 slices Texas toast
12 thin ham slices (about ½ oz. each)
1 tablespoon Dijon mustard
1 cup finely shredded Swiss cheese
6 eggs, beaten
2 cups milk
½ teaspoon ground nutmeg
2 cups finely shredded Cheddar cheese

6 servings

In small bowl, microwave margarine at 30% (Medium Low) for 15 to 45 seconds, or until softened. Lightly spread margarine on one side of each toast slice. Arrange 6 toast slices buttered-sides-up in 13 × 9-inch baking dish. Place 1 ham slice on each piece of toast. Spread ham evenly with mustard. Sprinkle evenly with Swiss cheese. Place remaining 6 ham slices over cheese. Top with remaining 6 toast slices, buttered-sides-down. Set aside.

In medium mixing bowl, combine eggs, milk and nutmeg. Pour evenly over sandwiches. Sprinkle evenly with Cheddar cheese. Cover with plastic wrap. Refrigerate 12 hours or overnight.

Heat conventional oven to 350°F. Remove plastic wrap. Cover with foil. Bake for 30 minutes. Remove foil. Bake for 15 to 20 minutes longer, or until puffed and golden brown.

Per Serving: Calories: 650 • Protein: 37 g.
• Carbohydrate: 48 g. • Fat: 34 g.
• Cholesterol: 294 mg. • Sodium: 1240 mg.
Exchanges: 2½ starch, 3½ medium-fat meat, ½ vegetable, ½ low-fat milk, 2½ fat

Reuben Strata ▲

Nonstick vegetable cooking spray
2 cups fresh broccoli flowerets
2 tablespoons water
6 eggs, beaten
3 cups milk
12 slices dark or light rye bread, cubed
2 cups shredded Swiss cheese
1 can (16 oz.) sauerkraut, rinsed and drained
1 pkg. (2.5 oz.) thinly sliced corned beef, cut into 2 × ½-inch strips
½ teaspoon salt

8 to 10 servings

Spray 13 × 9-inch baking dish with nonstick vegetable cooking spray. Set aside. In 2-quart casserole, combine broccoli and water. Cover. Microwave at High for 2 to 3 minutes, or until tender-crisp. Drain. Set aside. In large mixing bowl, combine eggs and milk. Add broccoli and remaining ingredients. Mix well. Spoon evenly into prepared baking dish. Cover with plastic wrap. Refrigerate 12 hours or overnight.

Heat conventional oven to 325°F. Remove plastic wrap. Cover with foil. Bake for 45 minutes. Remove foil. Bake for 25 to 30 minutes longer, or until knife inserted in center comes out clean. Let stand for 10 minutes before serving.

Per Serving: Calories: 270 • Protein: 18 g. • Carbohydrate: 23 g. • Fat: 12 g.
• Cholesterol: 161 mg. • Sodium: 790 mg.
Exchanges: 1 starch, 1½ medium-fat meat, 1½ vegetable, 1 fat

Egg & Sausage Bake

1 pkg. (12 oz.) frozen pork
   sausage links (12 sausages)
8 oz. fresh mushrooms, sliced
   (2 cups)
½ cup chopped green pepper
½ cup sliced green onions
2 tablespoons margarine or
   butter
1 pkg. (32 oz.) frozen loose-
   pack cubed hash browns
12 eggs, beaten
2 cups half-and-half
1 teaspoon salt
½ teaspoon pepper
½ teaspoon dried oregano
   leaves
1 cup shredded mozzarella
   cheese
1 cup shredded Cheddar
   cheese

8 to 10 servings

In 10-inch skillet, cook sausage links conventionally over medium-high heat for 8 to 12 minutes, or until hot and evenly browned. Drain. Set aside. In 2-quart casserole, combine mushrooms, green pepper, onions and margarine. Cover. Microwave at High for 4 to 6 minutes, or until vegetables are tender-crisp, stirring once.

Sprinkle hash browns evenly in 13 × 9-inch baking dish. Spoon mushroom mixture evenly over hash browns. Arrange sausage links over mushroom mixture. Set aside. In large mixing bowl, combine eggs, half-and-half, salt, pepper and oregano. Pour over sausages. Sprinkle evenly with cheeses. Cover with plastic wrap. Refrigerate 12 hours or overnight.

Heat conventional oven to 350°F. Bake, uncovered, for 1 hour 10 minutes to 1 hour 15 minutes, or until knife inserted in center comes out clean. Let stand for 10 minutes.

Per Serving: Calories: 430 • Protein: 22 g. • Carbohydrate: 22 g. • Fat: 28 g.
• Cholesterol: 313 mg. • Sodium: 820 mg.
Exchanges: 1 starch, 2 high-fat meat, 1½ vegetable, 2 fat

Greek Meat & Pasta Pie

- 2 tablespoons unseasoned dry bread crumbs
- 1 pkg. (7 oz.) uncooked elbow macaroni
- 1 lb. lean ground beef, crumbled
- ½ cup chopped onion
- 1 can (14½ oz.) diced tomatoes, drained

- 1 can (6 oz.) tomato paste
- ½ teaspoon salt
- ¼ teaspoon ground cinnamon
- ½ cup shredded fresh Parmesan cheese, divided
- 2 tablespoons margarine or butter
- 2 tablespoons all-purpose flour

- ⅛ teaspoon ground nutmeg
- 1 cup milk
- 2 eggs, beaten

6 to 8 servings

Per Serving: Calories: 330 • Protein: 20 g. • Carbohydrate: 30 g. • Fat: 15 g. • Cholesterol: 96 mg. • Sodium: 530 mg. Exchanges: 1½ starch, 2 medium-fat meat, 1½ vegetable, 1 fat

How to Make Greek Meat & Pasta Pie

Grease bottom and sides of 10-inch deep-dish pie plate. Sprinkle evenly with bread crumbs to coat. Set aside. Prepare macaroni as directed on package. Rinse and drain. Set aside. In 2-quart casserole, combine beef and onion.

Microwave at High for 4 to 7 minutes, or until meat is no longer pink, stirring twice to break apart. Drain. Add tomatoes, tomato paste, salt and cinnamon. Mix well. Spoon half of cooked macaroni evenly into prepared pie plate.

Spoon meat mixture evenly over macaroni. Using back of spoon, lightly pack meat mixture into plate. Sprinkle evenly with ¼ cup Parmesan cheese. Spoon remaining macaroni evenly over cheese. Set aside.

Place margarine in 2-cup measure. Microwave at High for 45 seconds to 1 minute, or until melted. Add flour and nutmeg. Mix well. Blend in milk. Microwave at High for 3 to 4 minutes, or until mixture thickens and bubbles, stirring twice.

Stir small amount of hot mixture gradually into eggs. Blend eggs back into hot mixture. Pour evenly over macaroni. Sprinkle evenly with remaining ¼ cup Parmesan cheese.

Cover with plastic wrap. Refrigerate 12 hours or overnight. Heat conventional oven to 350°F. Bake, uncovered, for 50 minutes to 1 hour, or until hot and lightly browned.

Pizza Manicotti

- 1 lb. Italian sausage, crumbled
- 1 can (28 oz.) whole tomatoes, undrained and cut up
- 1 can (15 oz.) pizza sauce
- 2½ cups shredded mozzarella cheese, divided
- 1 carton (15 oz.) ricotta cheese
- ½ cup halved pepperoni slices
- ½ cup snipped fresh parsley
- 1 egg
- 1 pkg. (8 oz.) uncooked manicotti shells (14 shells)
- 6 green pepper rings
- ¼ cup sliced black olives

8 servings

In 2-quart casserole, microwave sausage at High for 5 to 7 minutes, or until no longer pink, stirring twice to break apart. Drain. Add to-matoes and pizza sauce. Mix well. Set aside.

In medium mixing bowl, combine 1½ cups mozzarella cheese, the ricotta, pepperoni, parsley and egg. Stuff each uncooked manicotti shell evenly with mixture. Arrange stuffed shells in 13 × 9-inch baking dish. Spoon tomato mixture over shells. Arrange pepper rings over tomato mixture. Sprinkle evenly with olive slices. Cover with plastic wrap. Refrigerate 12 hours or overnight.

Heat conventional oven to 350°F. Remove plastic wrap. Cover with foil. Bake for 50 minutes to 1 hour, or until hot and bubbly. Remove foil. Sprinkle evenly with remaining 1 cup mozzarella cheese. Re-cover. Let stand for 5 minutes, or until cheese is melted.

Per Serving: Calories: 390 • Protein: 25 g. • Carbohydrate: 18 g. • Fat: 24 g.
• Cholesterol: 64 mg. • Sodium: 1150 mg.
Exchanges: 2½ medium-fat meat, 3½ vegetable, 2½ fat

Mexican Manicotti

½ cup chopped onion
2 cloves garlic, minced
2 cans (16 oz. each) pinto beans, rinsed and drained, divided
1 jar (16 oz.) salsa
1 carton (15 oz.) ricotta cheese
1½ cups shredded Monterey Jack cheese
½ cup snipped fresh parsley
1 egg
1 pkg. (8 oz.) uncooked manicotti shells (14 shells)
2 cups tomato juice
1 cup shredded Cheddar cheese
2 tablespoons canned chopped green chilies, drained

8 servings

In 2-quart casserole, combine onion and garlic. Cover. Microwave at High for 3 to 4 minutes, or until tender, stirring once. Add 1 can pinto beans and the salsa. Mix well. Set aside. In medium mixing bowl, combine remaining 1 can pinto beans, the ricotta, Monterey Jack cheese, parsley and egg. Stuff each uncooked manicotti shell evenly with mixture. Arrange stuffed shells in 13 × 9-inch baking dish. Spoon salsa mixture over shells. Pour tomato juice evenly over top. Cover with plastic wrap. Refrigerate 12 hours or overnight.

Heat conventional oven to 350°F. Remove plastic wrap. Cover with foil. Bake for 50 minutes to 1 hour, or until hot and bubbly. Remove foil. Sprinkle evenly with Cheddar cheese and chilies. Re-cover. Let stand for 5 minutes, or until cheese is melted.

Per Serving: Calories: 460 • Protein: 26 g.
• Carbohydrate: 50 g. • Fat: 17 g.
• Cholesterol: 77 mg. • Sodium: 880 mg.
Exchanges: 2 starch, 2 medium-fat meat, 4 vegetable, 1 fat

Greek Chicken & Spinach Bake

- 2 boneless whole chicken breasts (8 to 10 oz. each), skin removed, cut into ½-inch pieces
- ½ cup chopped onion
- 1 tablespoon dill seed
- 1 tablespoon dried parsley flakes
- ¼ teaspoon garlic powder
- 1 teaspoon vegetable oil
- 2 pkgs. (9 oz. each) frozen chopped spinach, defrosted
- 1 cup cottage cheese
- ½ cup crumbled feta cheese
- ⅓ cup margarine or butter
- 8 sheets frozen phyllo dough (18 × 14-inch sheets), defrosted, cut in half crosswise

8 servings

Per Serving: Calories: 250 • Protein: 23 g.
• Carbohydrate: 10 g. • Fat: 13 g.
• Cholesterol: 52 mg. • Sodium: 400 mg.
Exchanges: 3 lean meat, 2 vegetable, 1 fat

How to Make Greek Chicken & Spinach Bake

Combine chicken, onion, dill seed, parsley, garlic and oil in 2-quart casserole. Cover. Microwave at High for 5 to 7 minutes, or until meat is no longer pink, stirring 2 or 3 times.

Drain spinach, pressing to remove excess moisture. Add spinach, cottage cheese and feta cheese to chicken mixture. Mix well. Set aside.

Place margarine in small mixing bowl. Microwave at High for 1½ to 1¾ minutes, or until melted. Brush bottom and sides of 13 × 9-inch baking dish lightly with margarine.

Cheesy Confetti Corn Bake

- 4 oz. uncooked vermicelli, broken into 2-inch lengths
- ¼ cup plus 2 tablespoons margarine or butter, divided
- 2 cans (15 oz. each) cream-style corn
- 1 cup frozen corn
- 1 cup chopped green and red pepper
- 1 cup cubed fully cooked ham (½-inch cubes), optional
- 1 cup shredded Cheddar cheese
- ½ cup ready-to-serve chicken broth
- ¼ cup unseasoned dry bread crumbs

6 servings

In 2-quart casserole, combine vermicelli and ¼ cup margarine. Microwave at High for 4 to 5 minutes, or until lightly browned, stirring twice. Add remaining ingredients, except remaining 2 tablespoons margarine and the bread crumbs. Mix well. Cover. Refrigerate 12 hours or overnight.

Heat conventional oven to 350°F. In small mixing bowl, microwave remaining 2 tablespoons margarine at High for 45 seconds to 1 minute, or until melted. Add bread crumbs. Mix well. Sprinkle evenly over corn mixture. Bake conventionally, uncovered, for 55 minutes to 1 hour, or until casserole is hot and bubbly and topping is golden brown.

Per Serving: Calories: 430 • Protein: 16 g. • Carbohydrate: 50 g. • Fat: 20 g. • Cholesterol: 32 mg. • Sodium: 1030 mg. Exchanges: 3 starch, 1 lean meat, 1 vegetable, 3 fat

Unroll and remove phyllo sheets. Cover with plastic wrap. Place 1 half-sheet phyllo in prepared baking dish. Brush with melted margarine. Repeat layering 7 more times.

Spoon chicken mixture evenly over phyllo. Top with 1 half-sheet phyllo. Brush with melted margarine. Repeat layering 7 more times, brushing top with remaining margarine.

Cover with plastic wrap. Refrigerate 12 hours or overnight. Heat conventional oven to 350°F. Bake, uncovered, for 45 minutes to 1 hour, or until golden brown. Let stand for 10 minutes.

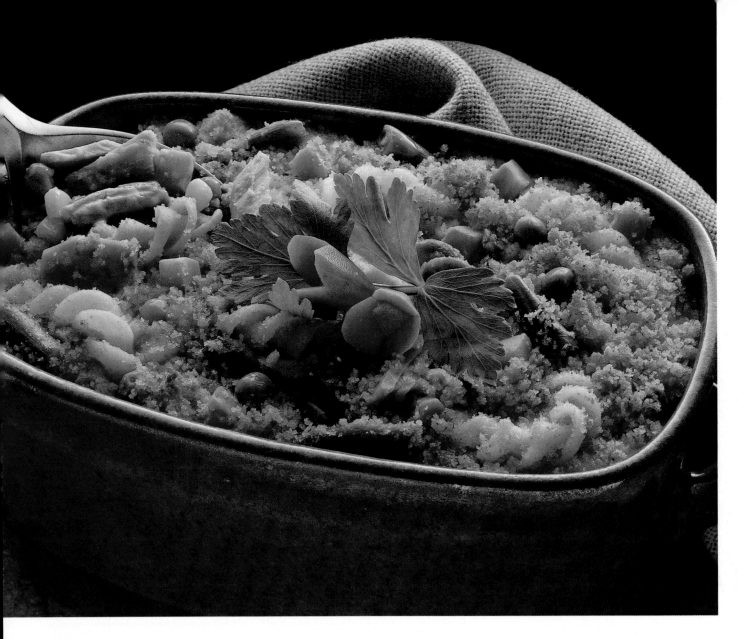

Easy Overnight Tuna Casserole

2 cups uncooked rainbow
   rotini
2 cups frozen mixed
   vegetables (any variety)
2 cans (10¾ oz. each)
   condensed cream of celery
   soup
1 cup shredded Cheddar
   cheese
1 cup milk
1 can (6½ oz.) solid white
   tuna, water pack, drained
   and flaked
2 tablespoons margarine or
   butter
½ cup unseasoned dry bread
   crumbs

4 to 6 servings

In 2-quart casserole, combine all ingredients, except margarine and bread crumbs. Cover. Refrigerate 12 hours or overnight.

In small mixing bowl, microwave margarine at High for 45 seconds to 1 minute, or until melted. Add bread crumbs. Toss to coat. Set aside. Microwave casserole at High, covered, for 12 to 15 minutes, or until mixture is hot, stirring 3 times. Sprinkle with bread crumb topping. Microwave at High, uncovered, for 2 minutes, or until hot.

TIP: To bake conventionally, heat oven to 350°F. Sprinkle with bread crumb topping. Bake, uncovered, for 55 minutes to 1 hour 10 minutes, or until hot and bubbly.

Per Serving: Calories: 410 • Protein: 22 g. • Carbohydrate: 43 g. • Fat: 17 g.
• Cholesterol: 39 mg. • Sodium: 1130 mg.
Exchanges: 2 starch, 1½ lean meat, 2½ vegetable, 2½ fat

Easy Overnight Seafood Bake

2 cups uncooked rainbow
  rotini

1 pkg. (9 oz.) frozen asparagus
  cuts

2 cans (10¾ oz. each)
  condensed cream of shrimp
  soup

1 cup shredded Cheddar
  cheese

1 cup milk

1 pkg. (10 oz.) frozen cooked
  tiny shrimp

2 tablespoons margarine or
  butter

½ cup unseasoned dry bread
  crumbs

4 to 6 servings

In 2-quart casserole, combine all ingredients, except margarine and bread crumbs. Cover. Refrigerate 12 hours or overnight.

In small mixing bowl, microwave margarine at High for 45 seconds to 1 minute, or until melted. Add bread crumbs. Toss to coat. Set aside. Microwave casserole at High, covered, for 12 to 15 minutes, or until mixture is hot, stirring 3 times. Sprinkle with bread crumb topping. Microwave at High, uncovered, for 2 minutes, or until hot.

TIP: To bake conventionally, heat oven to 350°F. Sprinkle with bread crumb topping. Bake, uncovered, for 55 minutes to 1 hour 10 minutes, or until hot and bubbly.

Per Serving: Calories: 400 • Protein: 24 g. • Carbohydrate: 38 g. • Fat: 16 g.
• Cholesterol: 129 mg. • Sodium: 1150 mg.
Exchanges: 2 starch, 2 lean meat, 1½ vegetable, 2 fat

Soups & Stews

Quick Vegetable & Lentil Chili

Soups & Stews: Techniques

Soups and stews may be the world's oldest form of a meal-in-a-pot. Versatile soups serve as light entrées or substantial meals. Some soups can be ready in minutes; others call for slow, attention-free simmering. The flavor of soups often improves with storage, making them a perfect choice for make-ahead meals. Store soups in the refrigerator for up to 2 or 3 days. For longer storage, ladle single or multiple servings of soup into freezer containers. Label and freeze for up to 3 months. To defrost soups, see the directions on pages 6 and 7.

Soup Toppers

Add distinction to soups with a garnish. A contrasting shape, texture, temperature or flavor appeals to both eye and appetite.

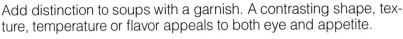

Crunchy:
chow mein noodles
cooked, crumbled bacon
crackers
crisp snack food: cheese balls,
   corn chips, pretzels, tortilla chips
crisp, unsweetened cereal
croutons
French-fried onions
popcorn
shoestring potatoes
sunflower nuts
toasted coconut
toasted nuts

Enriching:
cheeses, grated, shredded or
   cut out into shapes
dollop of sour cream or yogurt
hard-cooked egg, sieved or
   chopped

Fresh and colorful:
avocado slices
black or green olive slices
carrot, sliced or shredded
cucumber, sliced or shredded
green or red pepper, chopped
   or cut into strips
lemon, lime or orange slices
mushrooms, sliced or chopped
radish, sliced or shredded
sprouts (alfalfa or bean)
tomato, sliced or chopped

Flavor-enhancing:
dash of cayenne, chili powder,
   nutmeg or paprika
snipped fresh chives, parsley,
   basil, cilantro, dill or tarragon

Easy Soups for One, Two or Four

With a microwave oven, small or medium batches of "from scratch" soup can be ready in minutes. Microwaving times average about 5 minutes per serving. The recipes in this section limit additional preparation to minimize total work time.

Speed soup preparation by using some convenience foods, such as canned broth, Oriental dry noodle soup mix, instant rice or mashed potatoes, or canned tomatoes.

Prepare 1 or 2 servings of soup in a 4-cup measure, or to reduce cleanup, cook and serve single-serving soups in a 12-ounce bowl.

Choose a covered, 2-quart casserole for 4 servings. To keep the soup piping hot, carry the casserole hot from the oven to the table and serve family-style.

Embellish soups with one or two Soup Toppers (opposite) to complement the character of the soup.

Gazpacho for Two

½ cup seeded chopped
    tomato
½ cup finely chopped red
    pepper
¼ cup finely chopped onion
2 tablespoons olive oil
½ teaspoon dried dill weed
½ teaspoon sugar
¼ teaspoon salt
⅛ teaspoon freshly ground
    pepper
    Dash cayenne
1 can (6 oz.) tomato and chili
    cocktail
2 tablespoons red wine
    vinegar
1 cup seeded chopped
    cucumber

2 servings

In 4-cup measure, combine tomato, red pepper, onion, oil, dill weed, sugar, salt, pepper and cayenne. Cover with plastic wrap. Microwave at High for 4 to 8 minutes, or until vegetables are tender, stirring twice. In food processor or blender, process vegetable mixture until smooth. While food processor is running, slowly pour in tomato and chili cocktail and vinegar. Process until smooth. Stir in cucumber. Cover. Chill 2 hours.

Per Serving: Calories: 180 • Protein: 2 g. • Carbohydrate: 14 g. • Fat: 14 g.
• Cholesterol: 0 • Sodium: 610 mg.
Exchanges: 3 vegetable, 2½ fat

Quick Beer Cheese & Carrot Soup ▲

- 2 tablespoons shredded carrot
- 1 tablespoon finely chopped onion
- 1 tablespoon margarine or butter
- 2 tablespoons all-purpose flour
- 1 cup milk
- ½ cup pasteurized process cheese spread
- ¼ cup beer

1 serving

In 4-cup measure, combine carrot, onion and margarine. Microwave at High for 1½ to 2 minutes, or until vegetables are tender, stirring once. Stir in flour. Blend in milk, cheese and beer. Microwave at High for 3 to 3½ minutes, or until cheese can be stirred smooth and soup thickens and bubbles, stirring once.

Per Serving: Calories: 640 • Protein: 29 g. • Carbohydrate: 38 g. • Fat: 40 g. • Cholesterol: 81 mg. • Sodium: 1790 mg. Exchanges: 1 starch, 2 high-fat meat, 2 vegetable, 1 low-fat milk, 4 fat

Mexican Cheese Soup

- 2 tablespoons all-purpose flour
- 1 cup milk
- ½ cup frozen corn, red and green peppers
- ½ cup Mexican-flavored pasteurized process cheese spread
  Corn chips (optional)

1 serving

Place flour in 4-cup measure. Blend in milk. Add vegetables and cheese. Mix well. Microwave at High for 5 to 6 minutes, or until cheese can be stirred smooth and soup thickens and bubbles, stirring once. Garnish with corn chips.

Per Serving: Calories: 570 • Protein: 30 g. • Carbohydrate: 48 g. • Fat: 29 g. • Cholesterol: 81 mg. • Sodium: 1640 mg. Exchanges: 2 starch, 2 high-fat meat, 1 vegetable, 1 low-fat milk, 1½ fat

Cream of Chicken Noodle Soup

¼ cup thinly sliced celery
¼ cup thin carrot strips
     (1 × ⅛-inch strips)
 1 tablespoon margarine or
     butter
¼ teaspoon dried marjoram
     leaves
 1 pkg. (3 oz.) chicken-
     flavored Oriental dry
     noodle soup mix with
     seasoning packet
 1 tablespoon all-purpose flour
 2 cups hot water
 1 cup milk

              2 servings

In 4-cup measure, combine celery, carrot, margarine and marjoram. Cover with plastic wrap. Microwave at High for 4 to 5 minutes, or until vegetables are tender, stirring once. Stir in seasoning packet and flour. Blend in water and milk. Break up noodles and add to soup mixture. Microwave at High, uncovered, for 6 to 8 minutes, or until noodles are tender and soup is hot, stirring twice.

Per Serving: Calories: 320 • Protein: 9 g. • Carbohydrate: 37 g. • Fat: 15 g.
• Cholesterol: 23 mg. • Sodium: 980 mg.
Exchanges: 1½ starch, ½ vegetable, 1 low-fat milk, 2 fat

Oriental Spinach ▶ & Noodle Soup

3 cups hot water
1 cup frozen cut-leaf spinach
½ cup finely chopped fully cooked ham (optional)
1 pkg. (3 oz.) chicken-flavored Oriental dry noodle soup mix with seasoning packet

2 servings

In 4-cup measure, combine water, spinach and ham. Break up noodles. Add noodles and seasoning packet to mixture. Microwave at High for 6 to 10 minutes, or until noodles are tender and soup is hot, stirring once.

Per Serving: Calories: 200 • Protein: 7 g.
• Carbohydrate: 29 g. • Fat: 7 g.
• Cholesterol: 14 mg. • Sodium: 900 mg.
Exchanges: 1½ starch, ½ vegetable, 1 fat

Creamy Vegetable Rice Soup

1 packet (0.79 oz.) creamy chicken-flavored instant soup mix
1 cup frozen broccoli, carrots, water chestnuts and red pepper
3 tablespoons uncooked instant rice
1 cup hot water

1 serving

In 4-cup measure, combine soup mix, vegetables and rice. Stir in water. Microwave at High for 4 to 5 minutes, or until rice is tender and soup is hot, stirring once.

Per Serving: Calories: 220 • Protein: 5 g.
• Carbohydrate: 40 g. • Fat: 5 g.
• Cholesterol: 3 mg. • Sodium: 1120 mg.
Exchanges: 1½ starch, 3½ vegetable, 1 fat

Cream of Asparagus Soup ▲

- 1 pkg. (9 oz.) frozen asparagus cuts
- 1/2 cup chopped onion
- 1 tablespoon margarine or butter
- 1/4 cup all-purpose flour
- 1/4 teaspoon salt
- 1/8 teaspoon pepper
- 1 cup ready-to-serve chicken broth
- 1 cup milk or half-and-half
  Shredded carrot (optional)

4 servings

In 2-quart casserole, combine asparagus, onion and margarine. Cover. Microwave at High for 8 to 10 minutes, or until onion is tender, stirring twice. Stir in flour, salt and pepper. Blend in broth and milk. Microwave, uncovered, at 70% (Medium High) for 9 to 11 minutes, or until soup thickens and bubbles, stirring twice. (Do not boil.) Garnish each serving with shredded carrot.

Per Serving: Calories: 120 • Protein: 6 g. • Carbohydrate: 14 g.
• Fat: 5 g. • Cholesterol: 5 mg. • Sodium: 400 mg.
Exchanges: 1/2 starch, 1 1/2 vegetable, 1 fat

Instant Potato Corn Chowder

- 4 slices bacon, cut into 1/2-inch pieces
- 1 cup instant mashed potato flakes
- 1 cup frozen corn
- 1/2 cup finely chopped fully cooked ham
  (optional)
- 1/2 teaspoon salt
- 1/4 to 1/2 teaspoon pepper
- 2 cups milk or half-and-half

4 servings

Place bacon in 2-quart casserole. Cover with paper towel. Microwave at High for 5 to 6 minutes, or until bacon is brown and crisp, stirring once. Drain all but 1 tablespoon bacon drippings. Add potato flakes, corn, ham, salt and pepper. Mix well. Blend in milk. Microwave, uncovered, at 70% (Medium High) for 9 to 11 minutes, or until soup is hot, stirring twice. (Do not boil.)

Per Serving: Calories: 310 • Protein: 11 g. • Carbohydrate: 55 g.
• Fat: 6 g. • Cholesterol: 15 mg. • Sodium: 480 mg.
Exchanges: 3 starch, 1/2 low-fat milk, 1/2 fat

African Peanut Soup ▶

½ cup chopped green
  pepper
½ cup chopped onion
1 tablespoon vegetable oil
1½ teaspoons chili powder
1 can (14½ oz.) whole
  tomatoes, drained and
  cut up
1½ cups ready-to-serve
  chicken broth
1 can (8 oz.) tomato sauce
1 can (5 oz.) chunk breast of
  chicken, water pack,
  drained
¼ cup creamy peanut butter
1 teaspoon sugar
¼ cup chopped dry-roasted
  peanuts

4 servings

In 2-quart casserole, combine
green pepper, onion, oil and
chili powder. Cover. Microwave
at High for 3 to 5 minutes, or
until vegetables are tender, stirring once. Add remaining ingredients, except peanuts. Mix well.
Re-cover. Microwave at High
for 8 to 9 minutes, or until soup
is hot, stirring once or twice.
Garnish each serving with 1
tablespoon peanuts.

Per Serving: Calories: 310 • Protein: 18 g.
• Carbohydrate: 18 g. • Fat: 20 g.
• Cholesterol: 22 mg. • Sodium: 980 mg.
Exchanges: 1½ high-fat meat,
3½ vegetable, 1½ fat

Dilled Carrot Soup

12 medium carrots, thinly
  sliced (4 cups)
1 cup finely chopped onions
2 tablespoons olive oil
1 can (14½ oz.) ready-to-
  serve chicken broth
1 teaspoon dried dill weed
½ teaspoon salt
¼ teaspoon cayenne
  Sour cream (optional)

4 servings

In 2-quart casserole, combine carrots, onions and oil. Cover.
Microwave at High for 12 to 15 minutes, or until vegetables
are tender, stirring twice. In food processor or blender, process
vegetable mixture until smooth. While food processor is running, slowly pour in broth. Add dill weed, salt and cayenne.
Process until smooth. Pour puréed mixture back into 2-quart
casserole. Re-cover. Microwave at High for 6 to 8 minutes, or
until soup is hot. Garnish each serving with sour cream.

Per Serving: Calories: 150 • Protein: 4 g. • Carbohydrate: 16 g. • Fat: 8 g.
• Cholesterol: 0 • Sodium: 640 mg.
Exchanges: 3 vegetable, 1½ fat

Toasted Cheese & Tomato Soup

1/4 cup margarine or butter
1/4 teaspoon garlic powder
  4 cups fresh French bread
    cubes (3/4-inch cubes)
  1 can (10 3/4 oz.) condensed
    tomato soup
  1 can (14 1/2 oz.) whole
    tomatoes, undrained and
    cut up
1 1/4 cups water
  1 cup shredded Co-Jack
    cheese

4 servings

Heat conventional oven to 400°F. In medium mixing bowl, microwave margarine at High for 1 1/4 to 1 1/2 minutes, or until melted. Stir in garlic powder. Add bread cubes. Toss to coat. Place bread cubes in even layer on 15 1/2 × 10 1/2-inch baking sheet. Bake conventionally for 8 to 10 minutes, or until golden brown and crisp, stirring twice. In 2-quart casserole, combine soup, tomatoes and water. Cover. Microwave at High for 7 to 11 minutes, or until soup is hot, stirring twice. Ladle into 4 soup bowls. Top evenly with toasted bread cubes. Sprinkle evenly with cheese. Arrange bowls in microwave oven. Microwave at High for 2 to 3 minutes, or until cheese melts.

Per Serving: Calories: 410 • Protein: 13 g.
• Carbohydrate: 40 g. • Fat: 23 g.
• Cholesterol: 27 mg. • Sodium: 1260 mg.
Exchanges: 1 1/2 starch, 1/2 high-fat meat, 3 1/2 vegetable, 3 1/2 fat

Easy Italian Vegetable Soup

  1 cup thinly sliced zucchini
1/2 cup diced carrot
1/2 cup sliced fresh mushrooms
  1 tablespoon olive oil
  1 pkg. (0.7 oz.) Italian salad
    dressing mix

  1 can (16 oz.) whole tomatoes,
    undrained and cut up
  1 can (15 oz.) garbanzo
    beans, rinsed and drained
  1 can (14 1/2 oz.) ready-to-
    serve chicken broth

4 servings

In 2-quart casserole, combine zucchini, carrot, mushrooms and oil. Cover. Microwave at High for 5 to 6 minutes, or until vegetables are tender. Stir in dressing mix. Add remaining ingredients. Mix well. Re-cover. Microwave at High for 9 to 11 minutes, or until soup is hot, stirring once or twice.

Per Serving: Calories: 200 • Protein: 10 g. • Carbohydrate: 28 g. • Fat: 6 g.
• Cholesterol: 0 • Sodium: 1200 mg.
Exchanges: 1 starch, 3 vegetable, 1 fat

Beet & Potato Borscht

- 1 cup finely chopped onions
- 2 tablespoons margarine or butter
- 1 clove garlic, minced
- 1 can (16 oz.) diced beets, undrained
- 1 can (16 oz.) sliced potatoes, rinsed and drained
- 1 cup ready-to-serve chicken broth
- 1 teaspoon lemon juice
- ½ teaspoon salt
- ¼ teaspoon pepper
- ½ cup milk
- ¼ cup sour cream

4 servings

In 2-quart casserole, combine onions, margarine and garlic. Cover. Microwave at High for 4 to 6 minutes, or until onions are tender, stirring once. Add beets, potatoes, broth, juice, salt and pepper. Re-cover. Microwave at High for 8 to 11 minutes, or until mixture is hot, stirring once. Place beet mixture in food processor or blender. Add milk and sour cream. Process until mixture is smooth. Return to 2-quart casserole. Re-cover. Microwave at High for 2 to 3 minutes, or until soup is hot, stirring once.

Per Serving: Calories: 200 • Protein: 5 g.
• Carbohydrate: 24 g. • Fat: 10 g.
• Cholesterol: 9 mg. • Sodium: 1030 mg.
Exchanges: 1 starch, 2 vegetable, 2 fat

Fresh Vegetable Soup ▲

- 3 cups fresh vegetables, any combination (broccoli, carrots, cauliflower, onions, pea pods, peas, red and green peppers), cut into 1-inch chunks
- 2 cloves garlic, minced
- 1 teaspoon Italian seasoning
- 2 tablespoons olive oil
- 1 can (10½ oz.) condensed beef consommé
- 1 cup water
- ½ cup red wine
- ½ cup uncooked fine egg noodles

4 servings

In 2-quart casserole, combine vegetables, garlic, Italian seasoning and oil. Cover. Microwave at High for 4 to 7 minutes, or until vegetables are tender, stirring once. Blend in consommé, water, wine and noodles. Re-cover. Microwave at High for 9 to 10 minutes, or until noodles are tender and soup is hot, stirring twice.

Per Serving: Calories: 160 • Protein: 7 g. • Carbohydrate: 14 g. • Fat: 7 g.
• Cholesterol: 5 mg. • Sodium: 410 mg.
Exchanges: ½ starch, 1½ vegetable, 1½ fat

Soups for Six or More

Use a combination of conventional and microwave cooking to prepare soups in quantity. Large amounts of liquid and ingredients that need time to rehydrate take almost as long to microwave as they do to cook conventionally. Large pots are difficult to handle in the microwave oven; it's more convenient to let them simmer on the stove top. Legumes (beans, peas and lentils) require soaking to prepare them for cooking. When making legume soups, shorten preparation time by softening beans, peas and lentils in your microwave oven, as directed opposite.

Legumes are the richest source of vegetable protein. For full nutrition, complement legumes with a grain, such as rice, corn or wheat; or supplement them with small amounts of meat, fish or dairy products. The result is an inexpensive, vitamin and mineral-rich protein equal to animal protein in food value. As an energy food, low-fat, high-fiber legumes make a stick-to-the-ribs meal that satisfies hunger longer than other carbohydrates. Store dry beans, peas or lentils in moisture-proof containers in a cool, dry place. High temperature or humidity during storage may cause them to deteriorate. A 1-pound package of beans, peas or lentils contains about 2 cups of dry product, which yields 5 to 6 cups when cooked. If you wish to save time by using canned beans, a drained 15½-oz. can equals 1⅔ cups of cooked beans, or about ½ to ⅔ cup of dry beans.

Custom Soup Mixes

This section provides six legume or pasta soup and seasoning mixes you can assemble in advance, plus two different soup recipes for each mix. Supermarkets sell beans in 1 or 2-pound packages. For smaller amounts, as well as unusual varieties, shop in a co-op grocery that sells beans in bulk. While you're preparing the mixes, make up several batches for future use or to give as gifts. Package them in decorative containers, old-fashioned glass canning jars or plastic freezer bags.

How to Soften Beans, Peas & Lentils

Rinse and drain beans, peas or lentils; remove any grit and discolored or shriveled legumes. Place in 2-quart casserole.

Add 4 cups of water. Cover. Microwave at High for 8 to 15 minutes, or just until mixture begins to boil.

Let stand, covered, for 1 hour. Rinse and drain. Add to recipes as directed.

Mixed Pasta Soup & Seasoning Mix

1½ cups uncooked rainbow
    rotini (about 4 oz.)
 1 cup uncooked bow tie
    pasta (about 2 oz.)
 ½ cup uncooked macaroni
    rings (about 2 oz.)

Seasoning Mix:
 ¼ cup dehydrated vegetable
    flakes
 1 tablespoon instant chicken
    bouillon granules
 1 teaspoon bouquet garni
    seasoning
 1 teaspoon poultry
    seasoning
 1 teaspoon salt

Combine pastas in decorative jar or 1-pint food-storage bag. Combine all seasoning mix ingredients on sheet of plastic wrap. Fold wrap over seasoning mix to enclose. Place mix in jar or bag and seal. Store in cool, dry place, no longer than 6 months.

Grandma's Chicken & Pasta Soup ▲

 1 tablespoon vegetable oil
 ½ cup chopped onion
2½ to 3-lb. broiler-fryer
    chicken, cut up, skin
    removed
 8 cups water
 1 recipe Mixed Pasta Soup
    & Seasoning Mix (above)

                6 servings

In 6-quart Dutch oven or stock pot, heat oil conventionally over medium-high heat until hot. Add onions. Sauté for 2 to 3 minutes, or until onions are tender. Add chicken, water and seasoning mix. Bring soup mixture to boil over medium heat, stirring frequently. Reduce heat to low and simmer, partially covered, for 45 minutes to 1 hour, or until chicken is tender, stirring occasionally. Remove chicken from soup. Cool slightly. Cut chicken from bones. Discard bones. Set meat aside. Return mixture to boil over medium heat. Add pasta. Reduce heat and simmer for 10 to 14 minutes, or until pasta is tender, stirring occasionally. Add chicken to soup. Simmer, uncovered, for 3 to 5 minutes, or until soup is hot.

Per Serving: Calories: 280 • Protein: 23 g. • Carbohydrate: 30 g. • Fat: 8 g.
• Cholesterol: 54 mg. • Sodium: 610 mg.
Exchanges: 2 starch, 2½ lean meat

Hearty Minestrone Soup

2 tablespoons vegetable oil
1 lb. beef stew meat, cut into
   ½-inch pieces
1 cup sliced carrots
1 cup chopped celery
1 cup chopped onions
1 cup fresh green beans, cut
   into 2-inch lengths
8 cups water
¼ to ½ cup pesto
1 recipe Mixed Pasta Soup &
   Seasoning Mix (opposite)
1 can (28 oz.) whole tomatoes,
   drained and cut up
1 can (15 oz.) kidney beans,
   rinsed and drained
1 cup sliced zucchini

8 to 10 servings

In 6-quart Dutch oven or stock pot, heat oil conventionally over medium-high heat until hot. Add stew meat. Cook for 4 to 5 minutes, or until meat is brown, stirring frequently. Add carrots, celery, onions and green beans. Cook for 3 to 5 minutes, or until onions are tender, stirring frequently. Add water, pesto and seasoning mix. Bring soup mixture to boil over medium heat, stirring frequently. Reduce heat to low and simmer, partially covered, for 45 minutes to 1 hour, or until meat is tender, stirring occasionally. Return mixture to boil over medium heat. Add pasta, tomatoes, kidney beans and zucchini. Reduce heat and simmer for 15 to 20 minutes, or until pasta is tender and soup is hot, stirring occasionally.

Per Serving: Calories: 260 • Protein: 17 g. • Carbohydrate: 30 g. • Fat: 8 g.
• Cholesterol: 27 mg. • Sodium: 390 mg.
Exchanges: 1½ starch, 1 lean meat, 1½ vegetable, 1 fat

Curried Split Pea Soup & Seasoning Mix

 2 cups dried yellow or green
   split peas

Seasoning Mix:
 2 tablespoons instant
   vegetable bouillon granules
 2 tablespoons dehydrated
   vegetable flakes
 1 tablespoon curry powder
 1 teaspoon salt
 ½ teaspoon instant minced
   garlic

Combine peas in decorative jar
or 1-pint food-storage bag. Combine all seasoning mix ingredients on sheet of plastic wrap.
Fold wrap over seasoning mix
to enclose. Place mix in jar or
bag and seal. Store in cool, dry
place, no longer than 6 months.

◄ Curried Split Pea & Ham Soup

 1 recipe Curried Split Pea
   Soup & Seasoning Mix
   (above)
 6 cups water
 1½ cups cubed fully cooked
   ham (½-inch cubes)
 1 pkg. (10 oz.) frozen peas

                    6 to 8 servings

Soften split peas as directed,
page 121. In 6-quart Dutch oven
or stock pot, combine split peas,
seasoning mix and water. Bring
mixture to boil over medium
heat, stirring frequently. Reduce
heat to low and simmer, partially
covered, for 1¼ to 1½ hours, or
until split peas are softened,
stirring occasionally. Add ham
and peas. Continue to cook,
partially covered, for 15 to 30 minutes, or until soup is hot, stirring
occasionally.

Per Serving: Calories: 240 • Protein: 20 g.
• Carbohydrate: 37 g. • Fat: 2 g.
• Cholesterol: 14 mg. • Sodium: 1320 mg.
Exchanges: 2½ starch, 1 lean meat

Split Pea & Vegetable Black Bean Chowder

1 recipe Curried Split Pea Soup & Seasoning Mix (opposite)
2 tablespoons olive oil
1 lb. potatoes, cubed (1-inch cubes)
1 cup sliced carrots
1 cup sliced celery
6 cups water
2 medium zucchini, sliced (2 cups)
1 can (15 oz.) black beans, rinsed and drained
½ cup golden raisins

8 to 10 servings

Soften split peas as directed, page 121. Set aside. In 6-quart Dutch oven or stock pot, heat oil conventionally over medium-high heat until hot. Add potatoes, carrots and celery. Sauté for 4 to 5 minutes, or until vegetables are tender, stirring frequently. Stir in peas, seasoning mix and water. Bring mixture to boil over medium heat, stirring frequently. Reduce heat to low and simmer, partially covered, for 45 minutes to 1 hour, or until peas begin to soften, stirring occasionally. Add zucchini, black beans and raisins. Continue to cook, partially covered, for 30 to 45 minutes, or until peas are softened and zucchini is tender-crisp, stirring twice.

Per Serving: Calories: 270 • Protein: 14 g. • Carbohydrate: 48 g. • Fat: 4 g.
• Cholesterol: 0 • Sodium: 790 mg.
Exchanges: 2½ starch, 2 vegetable, ½ fat

Calico Bean Soup & Seasoning Mix

　2　cups mixed dried peas and beans (1/3 cup each of yellow and green split peas, lima beans, pinto beans, kidney beans and Great Northern beans)
1/3　cup uncooked barley

Seasoning Mix:
　1　tablespoon instant beef bouillon granules
　1　tablespoon dried celery flakes
　1　tablespoon dried parsley flakes
　1　teaspoon salt
1/2　teaspoon dried thyme leaves
1/2　teaspoon instant minced garlic
　5　whole peppercorns
　1　bay leaf

Combine peas, beans and barley in decorative jar or 1-pint food-storage bag. Combine all seasoning mix ingredients on sheet of plastic wrap. Fold wrap over seasoning mix to enclose. Place mix in jar or bag and seal. Store in cool, dry place, no longer than 6 months.

Barbecue Bean Stew ▲

　1　recipe Calico Bean Soup & Seasoning Mix (above)
　2　tablespoons vegetable oil
　2　cups sliced carrots
　1　cup sliced celery
　1　cup chopped onions
　5　cups water
　1　can (15 oz.) tomato sauce
　1　can (14 1/2 oz.) whole tomatoes, undrained and cut up
1/2　cup barbecue sauce
　1　tablespoon Worcestershire sauce

　　　　　　6 to 8 servings

Soften peas, beans and barley as directed, page 121. Set aside. In 6-quart Dutch oven or stock pot, heat oil conventionally over medium-high heat until hot. Add carrots, celery and onions. Sauté for 3 to 5 minutes, or until onions are tender. Add peas, beans and barley, seasoning mix and remaining ingredients. Bring mixture to boil over medium heat, stirring frequently. Reduce heat to low and simmer, partially covered, for 2 to 2 1/2 hours, or until beans are tender, stirring occasionally. Remove and discard bay leaf.

Per Serving: Calories: 250 • Protein: 12 g. • Carbohydrate: 44 g. • Fat: 5 g. • Cholesterol: 0 • Sodium: 990 mg.
Exchanges: 2 starch, 3 vegetable, 1 fat

Variation:
Barbecue Beef & Bean Stew: Prepare recipe as directed, except add 1 lb. beef stew meat, cut into 3/4-inch cubes, with vegetables. Cook for 4 to 5 minutes, or until meat is brown and onions are tender, stirring frequently. Continue to cook as directed, until meat and beans are tender.

Old-fashioned Vegetable Bean Soup

1 recipe Calico Bean Soup & Seasoning Mix (opposite)
2 tablespoons vegetable oil
1 lb. beef stew meat, cut into ¾-inch cubes
2 medium potatoes, peeled and cubed (¾-inch cubes)
2 medium carrots, sliced
2 ribs celery, sliced
½ cup chopped onion
6 cups water
1 can (28 oz.) whole tomatoes, undrained and cut up
1½ cups frozen corn
1 can (6 oz.) tomato paste

10 to 12 servings

Soften peas, beans and barley as directed, page 121. Set aside. In 6-quart Dutch oven or stock pot, heat oil conventionally over medium-high heat until hot. Add stew meat. Cook for 4 to 5 minutes, or until meat is brown, stirring frequently. Add potatoes, carrots, celery and onion. Cook for 3 to 5 minutes, or until onion is tender, stirring frequently. Add peas, beans and barley, seasoning mix and remaining ingredients. Bring mixture to boil over medium heat, stirring frequently. Reduce heat to low and simmer, partially covered, for 2 to 2½ hours, or until meat and beans are tender, stirring occasionally. Remove and discard bay leaf.

Per Serving: Calories: 240 • Protein: 17 g. • Carbohydrate: 35 g. • Fat: 5 g. • Cholesterol: 22 mg. • Sodium: 520 mg.
Exchanges: 1½ starch, 1 lean meat, 2½ vegetable, ½ fat

Cajun Soup & Seasoning Mix

- 1 cup dried black-eyed peas
- 1/2 cup dried lima beans
- 1/2 cup dried red kidney beans

Seasoning Mix:

- 1 tablespoon dried parsley flakes
- 1 1/2 teaspoons dried oregano leaves
- 1 1/2 teaspoons dried thyme leaves
- 1 teaspoon paprika
- 1 teaspoon instant chicken bouillon granules
- 1 teaspoon ground cumin
- 1/4 to 1/2 teaspoon cayenne
- 1/2 teaspoon instant minced garlic
- 1/2 teaspoon freshly ground pepper
- 1/2 teaspoon salt

Combine peas and beans in decorative jar or 1-pint food-storage bag. Combine all seasoning mix ingredients on sheet of plastic wrap. Fold wrap over seasoning mix to enclose. Place mix in jar or bag and seal. Store in cool, dry place, no longer than 6 months.

Hoppin' John Stew ▲

- 1 recipe Cajun Soup & Seasoning Mix (above)
- 1 tablespoon olive oil
- 1 1/2 cups chopped green peppers
- 1 cup sliced carrots
- 1 cup sliced celery
- 1 cup chopped onions
- 6 cups water
- 1 can (28 oz.) whole tomatoes, undrained and cut up
- 1 ham hock (about 1 lb.)
- 1/2 cup uncooked long-grain white rice

10 to 12 servings

Soften peas and beans as directed, page 121. Set aside. In 6-quart Dutch oven or stock pot, heat oil conventionally over medium-high heat until hot. Add green peppers, carrots, celery and onions. Sauté for 4 to 5 minutes, or until vegetables are tender, stirring frequently. Stir in peas and beans, seasoning mix, water, tomatoes and ham hock. Bring mixture to boil over medium heat, stirring frequently. Reduce heat to low and simmer, partially covered, for 1 hour 15 minutes, stirring occasionally. Stir in rice. Continue to cook, partially covered, for 30 to 45 minutes, or until rice and beans are tender, stirring occasionally. Remove ham hock from soup. Cool slightly. Cut ham from bone. Discard bone. Add ham to soup.

Per Serving: Calories: 180 • Protein: 11 g. • Carbohydrate: 31 g. • Fat: 2 g.
• Cholesterol: 6 mg. • Sodium: 390 mg.
Exchanges: 1 1/2 starch, 1/2 lean meat, 1 1/2 vegetable

Southern Succotash Soup

1 recipe Cajun Soup &
   Seasoning Mix (opposite)
1 tablespoon olive oil
1 cup sliced carrots
1 cup sliced celery
1 cup sliced onions
1 teaspoon salt
6 cups water
2½ to 3-lb. broiler-fryer
   chicken, cut up, skin
   removed
2 cups frozen corn
1 pkg. (9 oz.) frozen lima
   beans

      10 to 12 servings

Soften peas and beans as directed, page 121. Set aside. In 6-quart Dutch oven or stock pot, heat oil conventionally over medium-high heat until hot. Add carrots, celery and onions. Sauté for 4 to 5 minutes, or until vegetables are tender. Stir in peas and beans, seasoning mix, salt, water and chicken. Bring mixture to boil over medium heat, stirring frequently. Reduce heat to low and simmer, partially covered, for 1½ hours, stirring occasionally. Remove chicken from soup. Cool slightly. Cut chicken from bones. Discard bones. Add chicken, corn and lima beans to soup. Continue to cook, partially covered, for 30 to 45 minutes, or until beans are softened and soup is hot, stirring occasionally.

Per Serving: Calories: 240 • Protein: 20 g. • Carbohydrate: 32 g. • Fat: 5 g.
• Cholesterol: 33 mg. • Sodium: 360 mg.
Exchanges: 2 starch, 1½ lean meat, ½ vegetable

Black Bean & Bacon Soup ◀

  1 recipe Black Bean Soup &
      Seasoning Mix (left)
1/2 lb. bacon, cut into 1-inch
      pieces
  1 cup chopped red pepper
1/2 cup chopped onion
1/4 cup all-purpose flour
  8 cups water
  2 tablespoons red wine
      vinegar
1/2 cup sliced green onions

6 to 8 servings

Soften beans as directed, page
121. Set aside. In 6-quart Dutch
oven or stock pot, cook and stir
bacon over medium heat for 6
to 8 minutes, or until brown and
crisp. Remove bacon with slotted
spoon. Set aside. Drain and discard all but 2 tablespoons bacon
drippings. To drippings, add
red pepper and chopped onion.
Sauté over medium heat for 4
to 5 minutes, or until tender, stirring frequently. Stir in flour, beans,
seasoning mix and half of bacon.
Blend in water and vinegar. Bring
mixture to boil over medium heat,
stirring frequently. Reduce heat
to low and simmer, partially
covered, for 2 to 3 hours, or until
beans are softened and soup is
slightly thickened, stirring occasionally. Combine remaining
bacon with green onions. Garnish
each serving with bacon and
onion mixture.

Per Serving: Calories: 240 • Protein: 14 g.
• Carbohydrate: 38 g. • Fat: 5 g.
• Cholesterol: 7 mg. • Sodium: 410 mg.
Exchanges: 2 starch, 1/2 high-fat meat,
1 1/2 vegetable

Black Bean Soup & Seasoning Mix

  2 cups dried black beans

Seasoning Mix:
1/3 cup dried tomatoes, finely
      chopped
  2 teaspoons dried oregano
      leaves

  1 teaspoon paprika
  1 teaspoon salt
1/2 teaspoon pepper
  1 teaspoon instant minced
      garlic

Place beans in decorative jar or 1-pint food-storage bag. Combine
all seasoning mix ingredients on sheet of plastic wrap. Fold wrap over
seasoning mix to enclose. Place mix in jar or bag and seal. Store in
cool, dry place, no longer than 6 months.

Spicy Shrimp & Black Bean Chili

1 recipe Black Bean Soup &
   Seasoning Mix (opposite)
2 tablespoons olive oil
1 cup chopped green pepper
1 cup chopped onions
1 teaspoon chili powder
¼ teaspoon crushed red
   pepper flakes
6 cups water
1 can (14½ oz.) ready-to-
   serve chicken broth
1 lb. large shrimp, shelled
   and deveined
12 to 16 tortilla chips
½ cup finely shredded
   Cheddar cheese

     6 to 8 servings

Soften beans as directed, page 121. Set aside. In 6-quart Dutch oven or stock pot, heat oil conventionally over medium-high heat until hot. Add green pepper and onions. Sauté for 4 to 5 minutes, or until vegetables are tender, stirring frequently. Add beans, seasoning mix, chili powder, red pepper flakes, water and broth. Bring mixture to boil over medium heat, stirring frequently. Reduce heat to low and simmer, partially covered, for 2 to 3 hours, or until beans are softened, stirring occasionally. Stir in shrimp. Cook, uncovered, for 3 to 5 minutes, or until shrimp are firm and opaque. Remove from heat. Arrange tortilla chips in even layer on plate. Sprinkle evenly with cheese. Micro-wave at High for 30 to 45 seconds, or until cheese is melted. Garnish each serving of chili with 2 chips.

Per Serving: Calories: 320 • Protein: 23 g. • Carbohydrate: 38 g. • Fat: 9 g.
• Cholesterol: 72 mg. • Sodium: 580 mg.
Exchanges: 2 starch, 2 medium-fat meat, 1½ vegetable

Mixed Lentil Soup & Seasoning Mix

1 cup dried pink lentils
1 cup dried green lentils

Seasoning Mix:
1 tablespoon chili powder
1 tablespoon instant beef
   bouillon granules
1 tablespoon paprika

1 teaspoon ground cumin
1 teaspoon dry mustard
1 teaspoon dried oregano
   leaves
1 teaspoon sugar
1/2 teaspoon garlic powder
1/2 teaspoon dried lemon peel
1/2 teaspoon salt

Combine lentils in decorative jar or 1-pint food-storage bag. Combine all seasoning mix ingredients on sheet of plastic wrap. Fold wrap over seasoning mix to enclose. Place mix in jar or bag and seal. Store in cool, dry place, no longer than 6 months.

◀ Spicy Lentil & Sausage Chili

1 recipe Mixed Lentil Soup & Seasoning Mix (opposite)
2 tablespoons vegetable oil
1 cup chopped celery
1 cup chopped onions
3 cups water
2 cans (15 oz. each) tomato sauce
1 can (28 oz.) whole tomatoes, undrained and cut up
3/4 lb. seasoned bulk pork sausage

10 to 12 servings

Soften lentils as directed, page 121. Set aside. In 6-quart Dutch oven or stock pot, heat oil conventionally over medium-high heat until hot. Add celery and onions. Sauté for 2 to 3 minutes, or until vegetables are tender. Add lentils, seasoning mix, water, tomato sauce and tomatoes. Bring mixture to boil over medium heat, stirring frequently. Reduce heat to low and simmer, partially covered, for 30 minutes, stirring occasionally. Meanwhile, drop sausage by teaspoonfuls into 2-quart casserole. Microwave at High for 4 to 6 minutes, or until meat is no longer pink, stirring twice. Drain. Add to soup mixture. Continue to cook, partially covered, for 30 to 45 minutes, or until lentils are softened, stirring occasionally.

Per Serving: Calories: 230 • Protein: 14 g.
• Carbohydrate: 29 g. • Fat: 7 g.
• Cholesterol: 11 mg. • Sodium: 900 mg.
Exchanges: 1 starch, 1/2 high-fat meat, 3 vegetable, 1/2 fat

Quick Vegetable & Lentil Chili ▲

1 recipe Mixed Lentil Soup & Seasoning Mix (opposite)
2 tablespoons vegetable oil
1 cup chopped onions
2 cups cubed rutabaga (1/2-inch cubes)
2 carrots, cut into 1-inch lengths
1 cup diagonally sliced celery (1-inch chunks)
5 small new potatoes, cut into quarters (about 8 oz.)
2 1/4 cups water, divided
1 can (28 oz.) whole tomatoes, undrained and cut up
2 cans (15 oz. each) tomato sauce

10 to 12 servings

Soften lentils as directed, page 121. Set aside. In 6-quart Dutch oven or stock pot, heat oil conventionally over medium-high heat until hot. Add onions. Sauté for 2 to 3 minutes, or until onions are tender, stirring twice. Remove from heat. Set aside. In 2-quart casserole, combine rutabaga, carrots, celery, potatoes and 1/4 cup water. Cover. Microwave at High for 8 to 12 minutes, or until vegetables are tender, stirring twice. Drain. Add lentils, seasoning mix, vegetables, tomatoes, remaining 2 cups water and the tomato sauce to Dutch oven. Bring mixture to boil over medium heat, stirring frequently. Reduce heat to low and simmer, partially covered, for 1 to 1 1/4 hours, or until lentils are softened and vegetables are tender, stirring occasionally.

Per Serving: Calories: 210 • Protein: 12 g. • Carbohydrate: 36 g. • Fat: 3 g.
• Cholesterol: 0 • Sodium: 740 mg.
Exchanges: 1 1/2 starch, 2 1/2 vegetable, 1/2 fat

Fruited Chicken & Spinach Salad

Salad Bowl Meals: Techniques

Toss together a one-dish meal and eat the dish as well! Most of our attractive, full-meal salads have been combined with an edible bowl that complements the salad's flavors. The edible bowls are optional, so if you prefer, you can prepare and serve the salads in a natural container, a wooden or glass salad bowl or large mixing bowl.

Edible bowls featured in this section are Pancake, Bread, Egg Roll, Flour Tortilla and Tomato. For the Tropical Shrimp Salad, the pineapple shell serves as a natural container.

Salad Bowl Secrets

When preparing salad in a wooden or glass bowl, try one of these secrets:

- Rub inside of bowl with a cut garlic clove.
- Sprinkle inside of bowl with grated Parmesan cheese.
- Mix dressing in bowl and add salad ingredients to it.
- Prechill glass bowl for cold salads.
- Place salad bowl on platter; circle with garnishes.

Dry salad greens thoroughly before tossing in salad so dressing will cling to the leaves. Greens can either be dried in a salad spinner or placed between paper or cloth towels and patted dry.

Microwave-blanch vegetables such as broccoli, carrots, pea pods or peppers. Minimum cooking time is required to set color and eliminate raw taste. Rinse vegetables thoroughly under cold water to stop cooking and retain fresh, crisp texture.

Prevent discoloration of apples, avocados and bananas by dipping slices in a mixture of 2 cups water and 1 tablespoon lemon juice; or marinate them in salad dressing until ready to toss the salad.

Ham & Cheese Salad

Dressing:

¼ cup grated Parmesan cheese

¼ cup vegetable oil

2 tablespoons lemon juice

2 tablespoons white vinegar

2 tablespoons dried parsley flakes

1 teaspoon dry mustard

3 cups fresh broccoli flowerets

1 cup thinly sliced red onion

¼ cup water

4 cups leaf lettuce, torn into bite-size pieces

8 oz. fully cooked ham, cut into 2 × ¼-inch strips

1 cup Cheddar cheese curds

¾ cup string cheese, cut into 2-inch lengths

1 cup crisp cheese crackers

4 servings

In 2-cup measure, combine dressing ingredients. Set aside. In 2-quart casserole, combine broccoli, onion and water. Cover. Microwave at High for 3 to 4 minutes, or until broccoli is very hot and color brightens, stirring once. Rinse with cold water. Drain.

In large mixing bowl or salad bowl, combine broccoli and onion mixture, lettuce, ham, cheese curds and string cheese. Pour dressing over salad. Toss to coat. Add cheese crackers. Toss to combine. Serve in Bread Bowl (right), if desired. Serve immediately.

Per Serving: Calories: 550 • Protein: 34 g. • Carbohydrate: 22 g. • Fat: 37 g. • Cholesterol: 87 mg. • Sodium: 1320 mg. Exchanges: ½ starch, 4 lean meat, 3 vegetable, 5 fat

Bread Bowl

1 loaf (1 lb.) frozen white or whole wheat bread dough

1 egg white (optional) Sesame seed (optional)

1 bowl, 6 servings

Per Serving: Calories: 200 • Protein: 6 g. • Carbohydrate: 36 g. • Fat: 4 g. • Cholesterol: 4 mg. • Sodium: 360 mg. Exchanges: 2½ starch, ½ fat

How to Make Bread Bowl

Heat conventional oven to 350°F. Wrap loaf in greased sheet of wax paper or microwave cooking paper. Twist ends to seal. Microwave at 50% (Medium) for 2 minutes. Let stand for 5 minutes.

Turn over. Microwave at 50% (Medium) for 1 to 2 minutes, or until soft to the touch. Let stand to complete defrosting. Dough should remain cool. Shape dough into ball. Set aside.

Cover outside of 2-quart casserole with foil. Place foil-side-up on greased baking sheet. Stretch dough into 12-inch circle. Place over casserole, pressing and stretching to cover, forming 1-inch rim around edge.

Brush with egg white. Sprinkle with sesame seed. Bake conventionally for 25 to 30 minutes, or until golden brown. Cool completely. Loosen edges. Carefully lift bowl off casserole.

Turkey, Apple & Brie Cheese Salad

1 lb. fresh turkey breast slices
½ cup honey-mustard dressing, divided
6 cups torn fresh spinach leaves
8-oz. Brie cheese wheel, cut into 8 to 12 wedges
1 medium red apple, cored and cut into thin slices*
1 medium green apple, cored and cut into thin slices*
1 medium yellow apple, cored and cut into thin slices*
½ cup coarsely chopped walnuts

4 to 6 servings

Place turkey breast slices in 10-inch square casserole. Brush evenly with ¼ cup honey-mustard dressing. Cover with wax paper or microwave cooking paper. Microwave at High for 5 to 9 minutes, or until meat is no longer pink, rearranging slices twice. Let stand, covered, for 3 minutes. Cool slightly. Cut into 2 × ¼-inch strips.

In large mixing bowl or salad bowl, combine turkey, spinach, cheese, apples and walnuts. Toss to combine. Pour remaining ¼ cup dressing over salad. Toss to coat. Serve in Bread Bowl, page 138, if desired. Serve immediately.

*To prevent apples from discoloring, dip slices in mixture of 2 cups water and 1 tablespoon lemon juice.

Per Serving: Calories: 410 • Protein: 28 g.
• Carbohydrate: 18 g. • Fat: 26 g.
• Cholesterol: 97 mg. • Sodium: 450 mg.
Exchanges: 3½ lean meat, ½ vegetable, 1 fruit, 3 fat

Fruited Chicken & Spinach Salad

2   boneless whole chicken
    breasts (8 to 10 oz. each),
    split in half, skin removed
¼   cup apricot preserves
6   cups torn fresh spinach
    leaves
1   pint fresh strawberries,
    sliced (2 cups)
2   medium nectarines, sliced
1   avocado

Dressing:

¼   cup vegetable oil
¼   cup white wine vinegar
¼   cup apricot preserves
1   tablespoon poppy seed

4 servings

Place chicken in 8-inch square baking dish. Brush 1 tablespoon preserves over each chicken breast half. Cover with wax paper or microwave cooking paper. Microwave at High for 7 to 9 minutes, or until meat is no longer pink and juices run clear, rearranging once. Let stand, covered, for 3 minutes. Cool slightly. Cut into ½-inch pieces. Set aside.

In large mixing bowl or salad bowl, combine spinach, strawberries and nectarines. Using melon baller, scoop avocado into balls. Add to spinach mixture. Add chicken. Set aside.

In 2-cup measure, combine dressing ingredients. Microwave at High for 1 to 1½ minutes, or until mixture can be stirred smooth, stirring once. Add to spinach mixture. Toss to coat. Serve in Bread Bowl, page 138, if desired. Serve immediately.

Per Serving: Calories: 570 • Protein: 36 g. • Carbohydrate: 51 g. • Fat: 27 g.
• Cholesterol: 83 mg. • Sodium: 150 mg.
Exchanges: 4 lean meat, 1 vegetable, 3 fruit, 3 fat

Chinese Sprout & Snow Pea Salad

8 oz. fully cooked ham, cut into thin strips
8 oz. fresh bean sprouts
1 cup alfalfa sprouts
1 cup grated carrots
½ cup thinly sliced red onion
4 oz. fresh pea pods
2 tablespoons water

Dressing:

⅓ cup French dressing
1 tablespoon packed brown sugar
2 teaspoons soy sauce
1 teaspoon prepared mustard

4 servings

In large mixing bowl or salad bowl, combine ham, sprouts, carrots and onion. Set aside. In 1-quart casserole, place pea pods and water. Cover. Microwave at High for 1½ to 2½ minutes, or until pea pods are very hot and color brightens. Rinse with cold water. Drain. Add to salad mixture. In small mixing bowl, combine dressing ingredients. Add to salad. Toss to coat. Serve in Crispy Oriental Salad Bowls (below), if desired.

Per Serving: Calories: 240 • Protein: 16 g.
• Carbohydrate: 18 g. • Fat: 12 g.
• Cholesterol: 42 mg. • Sodium: 1170 mg.
Exchanges: ½ starch, 2 lean meat, 1 vegetable, ½ fruit, 1 fat

Crispy Oriental Salad Bowls

1 to 2 tablespoons vegetable oil
4 egg roll skins (7-inch)

4 bowls

Per Serving: Calories: 100 • Protein: 2 g.
• Carbohydrate: 9 g. • Fat: 6 g.
• Cholesterol: 0 • Sodium: 200 mg.
Exchanges: ½ starch, 1 fat

How to Make Crispy Oriental Salad Bowls

Heat conventional oven to 350°F. Invert four 10-oz. custard cups on large baking sheet with sides. Arrange cups at least 3 inches apart on baking sheet. Brush outsides of cups with oil.

Drape 1 egg roll skin over each custard cup. Brush lightly with oil. Bake for 12 to 15 minutes, or until golden brown. Cool completely. Carefully lift bowls off custard cups.

Sweet & Sour Ramen Noodle Salad

- 2 pkgs. (3 oz. each) Oriental dry noodle soup mix with seasoning packet (discard seasoning packets)
- 1 pkg. (2 oz.) slivered almonds
- 2 tablespoons sesame seed
- 1/3 cup margarine or butter
- 1 cup julienne carrot (2 × 1/4-inch strips)
- 1 cup red and green pepper chunks (1-inch chunks)
- 1 cup fresh broccoli flowerets
- 2 tablespoons water
- 1 boneless whole chicken breast (8 to 10 oz.), split in half, skin removed, cut into 1-inch pieces
- 4 cups shredded savoy cabbage
- 1/2 cup sliced green onions

Dressing:

- 1/3 cup vegetable oil
- 1/2 cup packed brown sugar
- 1/4 cup red wine vinegar
- 2 tablespoons soy sauce
- 1/4 teaspoon crushed red pepper flakes (optional)

4 servings

Finely crush noodles and place in small mixing bowl. Add almonds and sesame seed. Toss to combine. Set aside. In 8-inch skillet, melt margarine conventionally over medium heat. Add noodle mixture. Toss to coat. Cook and stir over medium heat for 5 to 7 minutes, or until golden brown. Set aside.

In 2-quart casserole, combine carrot, pepper chunks, broccoli and water. Cover. Microwave at High for 4 to 5 minutes, or until vegetables are very hot and color brightens. Rinse with cold water. Drain. Remove vegetables from casserole. Set aside.

Place chicken in same casserole. Cover. Microwave at High for 3 to 4 minutes, or until meat is no longer pink, stirring twice. Drain. In large mixing bowl or salad bowl, combine noodle mixture, vegetables and chicken. Add cabbage and onions. In small mixing bowl, combine dressing ingredients. Stir to dissolve sugar. Add to salad mixture. Toss to coat. Cover and chill 2 hours. Serve in Crispy Oriental Salad Bowls (opposite), if desired.

Per Serving: Calories: 780 • Protein: 27 g. • Carbohydrate: 67 g. • Fat: 47 g. • Cholesterol: 75 mg. • Sodium: 780 mg.
Exchanges: 1½ starch, 2 lean meat, 3 vegetable, 2 fruit, 8 fat

Ham, Swiss & Strawberry Salad with Orange Blossom Dressing

4 cups Bibb lettuce, torn into bite-size pieces
1 pint fresh strawberries, sliced (2 cups)
8 oz. fully cooked ham, cut into thin strips
1 medium orange, peeled, sliced and cut into bite-size pieces
4 oz. Swiss cheese, cut into thin strips (1 cup)
2 tablespoons margarine or butter
½ cup pecan halves

Dressing:

½ cup sour cream
2 tablespoons frozen orange juice concentrate, defrosted
1 tablespoon honey

4 servings

In large mixing bowl or salad bowl, combine lettuce, strawberries, ham, orange and cheese. Set aside. In 9-inch pie plate, melt margarine at High for 45 seconds to 1 minute. Add pecans. Toss to coat. Microwave at High for 2 to 3 minutes, or until pecans are hot, stirring after every minute. Add pecans to salad mixture. Toss gently to combine. Set aside. In small mixing bowl, combine dressing ingredients. Spoon evenly over salad. Toss to coat. Serve salad in Puffed Pancake Bowl (below), if desired.

Per Serving: Calories: 480 • Protein: 24 g. • Carbohydrate: 28 g. • Fat: 32 g. • Cholesterol: 69 mg. • Sodium: 840 mg. Exchanges: 3 lean meat, 1 vegetable, 1½ fruit, 4½ fat

Turkey Salad with Fresh Banana Dressing

Dressing:

1 medium banana, sliced
½ cup vanilla-flavored low-fat yogurt
1 tablespoon frozen orange juice concentrate, defrosted
1 tablespoon honey

1 lb. fresh turkey breast slices
6 cups torn mixed greens (Belgian endive, Bibb lettuce, leaf lettuce, radicchio and spinach)
1 pint fresh strawberries, sliced (2 cups)
2 kiwifruit, peeled, cut in half lengthwise and sliced
1 medium banana, sliced
2 medium oranges

4 to 6 servings

In food processor or blender, combine dressing ingredients. Process until smooth. Set aside. Place turkey breast slices in 10-inch square casserole. Cover with wax paper or microwave cooking paper. Microwave at High for 5 to 9 minutes, or until meat is no longer pink, rearranging slices twice. Let stand, covered, for 3 minutes. Cut into 2 × ¼-inch strips.

In large mixing bowl or salad bowl, combine turkey, greens, strawberries, kiwifruit and banana. Using sharp knife, cut peel and white membrane from oranges. Slice oranges crosswise into ¼-inch slices. Cut slices in half. Add to salad. Toss to combine. Serve salad in Puffed Pancake Bowl (below), if desired. Serve with dressing.

Per Serving: Calories: 220 • Protein: 21 g. • Carbohydrate: 33 g. • Fat: 1 g. • Cholesterol: 48 mg. • Sodium: 60 mg. Exchanges: 2 lean meat, ½ vegetable, 2 fruit

Puffed Pancake Bowl

2 eggs, beaten
½ cup all-purpose flour
½ cup milk
2 tablespoons margarine or butter

1 bowl, 4 servings

Per Serving: Calories: 160 • Protein: 6 g. • Carbohydrate: 14 g. • Fat: 9 g. • Cholesterol: 109 mg. • Sodium: 115 mg. Exchanges: 1 starch, ½ medium-fat meat, 1 fat

How to Make Puffed Pancake Bowl

Heat conventional oven to 425°F. In medium mixing bowl, beat together eggs, flour and milk with whisk. Set batter aside. Place margarine in 10-inch deep-dish pie plate. Place in oven to melt.

Tilt pie plate to coat bottom and sides. Pour batter into pie plate. Bake for 17 to 20 minutes, or until pancake bowl is puffed and edges are golden brown. Serve immediately.

Fiesta Flour Tortilla Bowls

Vegetable oil
4 flour tortillas (8-inch)

4 bowls

Per Serving: Calories: 170 • Protein: 3 g. • Carbohydrate: 25 g. • Fat: 7 g.
• Cholesterol: 0 • Sodium: 200 mg.
Exchanges: 1½ starch, 1½ fat

How to Make Fiesta Flour Tortilla Bowls

Heat conventional oven to 350°F. Invert four 10-oz. custard cups on large baking sheet with sides. Arrange cups at least 3 inches apart on baking sheet.

Heat ⅛ inch oil conventionally over medium-high heat in 10-inch skillet. Dip both sides of each tortilla in hot oil to moisten.

Drape 1 tortilla over each custard cup. Bake for 10 to 12 minutes, or until tortillas begin to brown lightly. Cool completely. Carefully lift tortilla bowls off custard cups.

◄ Southwestern Chicken & Rice Salad

1 cup uncooked long-grain white rice

Dressing:

⅓ cup lemon juice
⅓ cup olive oil
¼ cup sliced green onions
1 teaspoon dried cilantro leaves or 1 tablespoon snipped fresh cilantro leaves
⅛ teaspoon cayenne
Pinch crushed red pepper flakes

2 boneless whole chicken breasts (8 to 10 oz. each), split in half, skin removed
2 cups frozen corn
3 tablespoons water
3 cups shredded leaf lettuce
1 cup julienne jicama (2 × ¼-inch strips), optional
1 cup chopped red and green peppers

4 servings

Prepare rice as directed on package. Set aside. In 1-cup measure, combine dressing ingredients. Place chicken breast halves in 10-inch square casserole. Drizzle ¼ cup dressing over chicken. Cover. Set remaining dressing aside. Microwave at High for 7 to 9 minutes, or until meat is no longer pink and juices run clear, rearranging once. Let stand, covered, for 3 minutes. Cut into ½-inch pieces. Set aside. In 3-quart casserole, combine corn and water. Cover. Microwave at High for 6 to 8 minutes, or until corn is defrosted, stirring once. Drain. Add rice, remaining ½ cup dressing, the chicken, lettuce, jicama and chopped peppers. Toss to combine. Serve salad warm. Serve in Fiesta Flour Tortilla Bowls (opposite), if desired.

Per Serving: Calories: 580 • Protein: 37 g.
• Carbohydrate: 59 g. • Fat: 23 g.
• Cholesterol: 83 mg. • Sodium: 85 mg.
Exchanges: 3 starch, 3½ lean meat, 3 vegetable, 2 fat

Vera Cruz Tuna Salad ▲

2 cups uncooked elbow macaroni
1 cup shredded Cheddar cheese, divided
1 can (6½ oz.) solid white tuna, water pack, drained and flaked
1 can (4 oz.) chopped green chilies

½ cup mayonnaise or salad dressing
½ cup seeded chopped tomato
½ cup chopped celery
⅓ cup sliced green onions
⅓ cup sliced pitted black olives

4 servings

Prepare macaroni as directed on package. Rinse and drain. Place in large mixing bowl or 2-quart casserole. Add ½ cup cheese and the remaining ingredients. Mix well. Microwave at 50% (Medium) for 8 to 11 minutes, or until warm, stirring twice. Sprinkle with remaining ½ cup cheese. Microwave at 50% (Medium) for 4 to 5 minutes, or until cheese is melted. Serve salad warm. Serve in Fiesta Flour Tortilla Bowls (opposite), if desired.

Per Serving: Calories: 590 • Protein: 27 g. • Carbohydrate: 45 g. • Fat: 34 g.
• Cholesterol: 54 mg. • Sodium: 930 mg.
Exchanges: 2 starch, 2 lean meat, 3 vegetable, 5½ fat

Curry Chicken Salad Stuffed Tomatoes

4 medium tomatoes (8 oz. each)

¼ cup plus 1 tablespoon vegetable oil, divided

2 teaspoons sugar

2½ teaspoons curry powder, divided

½ teaspoon salt

4 oz. uncooked macaroni shells (1 cup)

2 boneless whole chicken breasts (8 to 10 oz. each), split in half, skin removed

½ cup chopped celery

½ cup chopped green pepper

2 tablespoons water

4 green onions, diagonally sliced (¾-inch slices)

4 servings

Cut thin slice from top of each tomato. Scoop out and discard pulp and seeds, leaving ¼-inch shells. Set aside. In 1-cup measure, combine ¼ cup oil, the sugar, 1½ teaspoons curry powder and the salt. Set dressing aside. Prepare macaroni as directed on package. Rinse with cold water. Drain. Set aside.

Place chicken in 8-inch square baking dish. In small bowl, combine remaining 1 tablespoon oil and 1 teaspoon curry powder. Brush evenly over chicken. Cover with wax paper or microwave cooking paper. Microwave at High for 7 to 9 minutes, or until meat is no longer pink and juices run clear, rearranging twice. Let stand, covered, for 3 minutes. Cut into ½-inch pieces. Set aside.

In 2-quart casserole, combine celery, green pepper and water. Cover. Microwave at High for 2 to 3 minutes, or until vegetables are tender-crisp. Drain. Add dressing, macaroni, chicken and onions. Toss to coat. Spoon salad evenly into tomato shells.

Per Serving: Calories: 460 • Protein: 36 g. • Carbohydrate: 32 g. • Fat: 22 g.
• Cholesterol: 83 mg. • Sodium: 370 mg.
Exchanges: 1 starch, 3½ lean meat, 3½ vegetable, 2 fat

Tortellini & Ham Salad Stuffed Tomatoes

- 4 medium tomatoes (8 oz. each)
- 1 pkg. (9 oz.) uncooked fresh cheese tortellini
- 3 cups fresh broccoli flowerets
- 2 tablespoons water
- 1½ cups cubed fully cooked ham (½-inch cubes)
- 1 jar (6½ oz.) marinated quartered artichoke hearts, undrained and cut up
- ½ cup snipped fresh parsley
- ½ cup Italian dressing
- 1 jar (2 oz.) sliced pimientos, drained
- ¼ cup grated Parmesan cheese
- ¼ teaspoon dried basil leaves

4 servings

Cut thin slice from top of each tomato. Scoop out and discard pulp and seeds, leaving ¼-inch shells. Set aside. Prepare tortellini as directed on package. Rinse with cold water. Drain. Set aside.

Place broccoli and water in 2-quart casserole. Cover. Microwave at High for 3 to 4 minutes, or until broccoli is tender-crisp, stirring once. Rinse with cold water. Drain. In large mixing bowl or salad bowl, combine tortellini, broccoli and remaining ingredients, except tomato shells. Toss to combine. Spoon salad evenly into tomato shells.

Per Serving: Calories: 560 • Protein: 29 g. • Carbohydrate: 49 g. • Fat: 30 g. • Cholesterol: 68 mg. • Sodium: 1440 mg. Exchanges: 2 starch, 2 lean meat, 4 vegetable, 4½ fat

Seashell Louis Salad

4 oz. uncooked shell
    macaroni (1 cup)

Dressing:

½ cup mayonnaise
2 tablespoons whipping
    cream
2 tablespoons chili sauce
2 tablespoons chopped
    green pepper
2 tablespoons sliced green
    onion
1 tablespoon lemon juice
½ teaspoon Worcestershire
    sauce

1 pkg. (9 oz.) frozen peas
2 tablespoons water
1 pkg. (8 oz.) seafood sticks,
    cut into ¾-inch pieces
    Large outer leaves from
    head of Bibb lettuce
1 medium tomato, cut into
    8 wedges
1 lemon, cut into 8 wedges

4 servings

Prepare macaroni as directed
on package. Rinse with cold
water. Drain. Set aside. In medium mixing bowl or salad bowl,
combine dressing ingredients.
Set aside. In 1-quart casserole,
combine peas and water. Cover.
Microwave at High for 3 to 5
minutes, or until peas are defrosted, stirring once. Rinse with
cold water. Drain. Add macaroni,
peas and seafood sticks to dressing. Toss to coat. On each of 4
individual serving plates, arrange
lettuce leaves to form bowls, or
line Fiesta Flour Tortilla Bowls,
page 146, with lettuce. Spoon
salad evenly into each. Garnish
with tomato and lemon wedges.

Per Serving: Calories: 460 • Protein: 17 g.
• Carbohydrate: 41 g. • Fat: 26 g.
• Cholesterol: 44 mg. • Sodium: 440 mg.
Exchanges: 2½ starch, 1 lean meat,
1 vegetable, 4½ fat

Chick Pea & Cucumber Tabbouleh

1½ cups water
¾ cup uncooked bulgur or
    cracked wheat

Dressing:

¼ cup fresh lemon juice
¼ cup olive oil
2 tablespooons red wine
    vinegar
2 teaspoons dried mint leaves
½ teaspoon salt
¼ teaspoon pepper
⅛ teaspoon cayenne

2 cups green and red pepper
    strips (2 × ¼-inch strips)
1 tablespoon olive oil
1 clove garlic, minced
1 can (16 oz.) garbanzo
    beans (chick peas), rinsed
    and drained
1 medium tomato, seeded
    and chopped (1 cup)
1 cup coarsely chopped
    cucumber
½ cup snipped fresh parsley
¼ cup sliced green onions
    Romaine lettuce leaves

4 servings

Per Serving: Calories: 390 • Protein: 11 g. • Carbohydrate: 48 g. • Fat: 19 g.
• Cholesterol: 0 • Sodium: 290 mg.
Exchanges: 2½ starch, 2 vegetable, 3½ fat

How to Microwave Chick Pea & Cucumber Tabbouleh

Place water in 4-cup measure.
Microwave at High for 2½ to
3½ minutes, or until it begins
to boil. Add bulgur. Cover with
plastic wrap. Let stand for 30
minutes, or until all water is absorbed. In 1-cup measure,
combine dressing ingredients.
Set aside. In 2-quart casserole,
combine pepper strips, oil and
garlic. Cover. Microwave at High
for 2 to 3 minutes, or until pepper strips are tender-crisp, stirring once.

Add bulgur, beans, tomato,
cucumber, parsley and onions.
Pour dressing over salad mixture. Toss to combine. Cover
and chill 4 to 6 hours, or until
flavors are blended. On each
of 4 individual serving plates,
arrange romaine leaves to form
bowls, or line Fiesta Flour Tortilla Bowls, page 146, with lettuce.
Spoon salad evenly into each.

Tropical Shrimp Salad

- 1 lb. medium shrimp, shelled and deveined
- 1 fresh pineapple (4 lbs.)
- 3 cups cooked long-grain white rice
- 1 can (11 oz.) mandarin orange segments, drained
- 1 mango or papaya, cut into 1-inch chunks
- 4 green onions, diagonally sliced (1-inch slices)
- 3 tablespoons cream of coconut
- 2 tablespoons mayonnaise
- 1 tablespoon lime juice
- ½ to 1 teaspoon grated fresh gingeroot

4 to 6 servings

Per Serving: Calories: 300 • Protein: 15 g.
• Carbohydrate: 47 g. • Fat: 7 g.
• Cholesterol: 89 mg. • Sodium: 120 mg.
Exchanges: 1½ starch, 1½ lean meat,
½ vegetable, 1½ fruit, ½ fat

How to Microwave Tropical Shrimp Salad

Arrange shrimp in single layer in 10-inch square casserole. Cover. Microwave at 70% (Medium High) for 5 to 8 minutes, or until shrimp are firm and opaque, stirring once. Drain. Set aside.

Cut pineapple in half lengthwise, leaving leafy portions attached. With thin, flexible knife, loosen and remove fruit, leaving ½-inch shells. Cover shells with plastic wrap. Place in refrigerator.

Cut and discard core from pineapple. Cut fruit into 1-inch chunks.

Combine rice, shrimp, pineapple, orange segments, mango and onions in medium mixing bowl. Set aside.

Combine remaining ingredients in 1-cup measure. Pour over shrimp mixture. Toss to coat. Chill about 4 hours or overnight. Serve in pineapple shells.

Index